From Geelong to Gallipoli — And Back: 1914–1919
The Story of Two Geelong Brothers During World War 1

Researched and compiled by Wendy Hebbard (nee Gollan) — niece of Herbert Roy Gollan
Copyright © Wendy Hebbard 2022

ISBN: 978-0-9944362-3-8

First published 2022

All rights reserved. Without limiting the rights under copyright reserved above, no part of this publication may be reproduced, stored in or introduced into a database and retrieval system or transmitted in any form or any means (electronic, mechanical, photocopying, recording or otherwise) without the prior written permission of the owner of copyright.

Design & editing by PBPublishing
Gisborne Victoria
www@pbpublishing.com.au

Printed in Melbourne, Victoria

DEDICATED TO

Bruce Gollan (New Zealand)
Harry and Robert Gollan (dec'd)
Ern Gollan (dec'd)

ACKNOWLEDGEMENTS

With sincere thanks to all those who assisted in producing this book, including Phillipa Butler for layout and design and to my husband Ron Hebbard for his support and encouragement.

Wendy Hebbard

PREFACE

This account covers two Gollan brothers who served in World War I, and some of their Geelong compatriots. The brothers were both decorated by the British Government. Both returned to their homes, with wounds, and settled back into Australian life.

The elder, HR Gollan — Herbert Roy — was known as Roy. He was a reporter for the 'Geelong Advertiser' and 'News of the Week'—an adjunct to the 'Advertiser' which published soldiers' letters. Much of the included material is from Roy's reports to the papers. It made interesting but often sad reading. Here are many of his letters from Gallipoli and the Western Front. When scanning these old newspaper pages, the eye caught many stories of other Geelong boys. Some fascinating sidelines, often tragic, but Roy did not actually report very much of the horrors and hardships that he witnessed — quite possibly the material was censored.

Younger brother R W Gollan — Robert Wilson (Bert) — does not feature as largely in the stories. He must also have been a letter writer however because it is reported that on one occasion in the trenches he received a backlog of 50 letters.

Roy and Bert had a happy meeting in Paris and a lovely photo of that time is captured by the camera.

From 'The Age', Melbourne —
'THE WAR TO END ALL WARS'
"World War 1 (1914-18) remains Australia's most costly conflict in terms of deaths and casualties.
    300,000 men enlisted from a population of 4.97 million.
    More than 60,000 were killed and 150,000 wounded or taken prisoner.
    Australians and New Zealanders landed at what became known as Anzac Cove on April 25, 1915.

8709 Australians died at Gallipoli (Turkish name Gelibolu).
After the evacuation from Gallipoli (December 19-20, 1915), the men were progressively transferred to France. The war on the Western Front was at a stalemate, with the opposing armies facing each other from trenches which extended across Belgium and north-western France.

Australian infantry were introduced to this type of warfare at Fromelles, in July 1916 suffering 5533 casualties in 24 hours.
From 1916-18, 48,671 Australians died on the Western Front.

Unlike their counterparts in France and Belgium, Australian troops in the Middle East — the Light Horsemen and their mounts — fought a mobile war in extreme heat, harsh terrain and water shortages; 1394 soldiers were killed or wounded in three years of war.

Source Australian War Memorial"

CONTENTS

Introduction – Roy Gollan 1

War Hero – Roy Gollan 3

The Beginning 7

Roy Gollan – Letters – 1915–16 9

Robert Wilson Gollan 62

Letters in 'News of The Week'
('Geelong Advertiser') – 1917 64

Roy Gollan – War Record Summary 82

A Life in India 91

INTRODUCTION ~ ROY GOLLAN

Destined to become a renowned citizen and wartime hero, Herbert Roy Gollan was the first child of Harriett Wilson and Robert Harper Gollan (married 1891). Roy was born in Gawler, South Australia, on 29 August 1892.

His parents, who were Salvation Army officers, were married in the Melbourne Exhibition Buildings at a mass ceremony conducted by General William Booth, the founder of the Salvation Army.

The Gollans lived for a time in Geelong and then in Brunswick, where Robert ran a wood merchant's business as well as conducting his Salvation Army duties. They lived by faith and were supported by other believers. Harriett remembered one occasion when there was no food to feed the family for dinner. Just then, there was a knock at the door and someone arrived with a hot meal for them.

Eventually three more children came along: Robert, Ernest and Elsie.

Roy was determined to get on. He was a reporter for the 'Hamilton Spectator, the Melbourne 'Argus' and the 'Geelong Advertiser', and was later employed by the Tourist Bureau. After World War I, he was appointed Australian Trade Commissioner in India. He wrote that he saw great possibilities for Australian trade with that country.

As a reporter for the 'Geelong Advertiser', he wrote many letters and reports back from the theatres of war, where he served with distinction, being awarded high honours. Roy's letters appeared regularly during the war in the 'News of the Week' — an adjunct to the 'Advertiser'.

In the beginning, Roy is part of a big send-off and street parade as the "boys" march off to the training camp.

We have letters from him on the ship and then from camp in Egypt before the troops sailed for Gallipoli. Roy became ill at Gallipoli and eventually ended up at an officers' training centre in England, then was sent across to the Western Front. Luckily he was able to make contact with his brother, Robert.

While a good officer, his rapid promotion to the rank of Major illustrates that the attrition rate was high in the battlefield.

Both brothers eventually returned—Robert (Bert) to New Zealand and Roy to Melbourne to marry Muriel Hyatt and move on to become the Australian High Commissioner in India.

Roy's exploits on the battlefield saw him highly decorated, but no particular act of gallantry was recorded. He proved himself to be an inspiring leader of men and an extraordinarily capable organiser of supplies, working under pressure.

As High Commissioner, he moved easily in elite circles. One humorous incident is remembered in the family. When he and his wife Muriel arrived to perform duties in one large Indian city, a street parade welcome was organised. Banners were stretched across the road.

"GOD BLESS MR GOLLAN" read the first one. When Muriel's car followed, the second banner read: "GOD HELP MRS GOLLAN" *(told by Lilian Gollan).*

They returned to Melbourne in the late 1950s.

Roy Gollan was the uncle of Wendy Hebbard.

June 12, 2019

WAR HERO ~ ROY GOLLAN

"It's a nice house on the Esplanade, overlooking the Bay in Geelong," boasted Rosemary to her friends.

But it wasn't anything of the sort. The small house her grandparents' family lived in at the beginning of the 20th century was a tiny worker's cottage in Elizabeth Street, West Geelong.

Harriet prayed for each of her four children every day of her long life. When she passed away in her late eighties, her children had made her proud indeed. Two sons were highly-decorated heroes in the First World War, the youngest son had travelled widely around the world on a motorbike in the 1920s when that sort of thing was practically unheard of, and her daughter had been loving and faithful, an excellent cook and home-maker.

The whole family worshipped at the Aberdeen Street Baptist Church when it was surely in its heyday.

On Sunday evenings they sang around the piano in the front room of their home. The boys were of course respectable, but prided themselves in being among the Pako gang.

Herbert Roy enlisted at the Geelong Recruitment Centre in 1914 at the age of twenty, having worked as a reporter for the 'Geelong Advertiser'. His brother, Robert, also enlisted there a few weeks later.

Roy, as he was known, shipped out to Egypt, then to the Gallipoli Peninsula in 1915. He contracted typhoid and was invalided to the island of Malta.

He was transferred to the battle lines of France and sustained a gunshot wound to the chest which put him back in hospital in England.

Showing promise as an administrator, Roy received some Army college training in England then returned to the front line.

He rose quickly through the ranks, becoming in time a Brigade Major. One incident, for which he received a high distinction, involved "leapfrogging" his brigade across to the front line over another battalion and facing heavy enemy fire whilst waiting for the Canadians to back him up. The expected tanks did not arrive. The Brigadier of the 6th Canadian Infantry wrote that "their prompt and generous action enabled our assault to proceed in this initial stage and saved us numerous casualties."

By the end of the war, Roy had been awarded the Military Cross and the DSO, and had twice been mentioned in despatches by General Haigh.

After serving as Managing Editor of the now-defunct 'Argus' and the 'Australasian' newspapers, and founding another one — 'The Star' — Roy entered the Diplomatic Corps.

His most esteemed position was when he became Australian High Commissioner in India. His ability to get on well with men and to inspire them, as well as his high organising ability, made him a man of great calibre, one of Geelong's proudest sons.

Herbert Roy Gollan

The Gollan family. (L-R): Ernest (Ern), Robert senior, Roy, Elsie, Harriet and Bert.

The three Gollan boys, 1903: Ern, Roy and Bert.

THE BEGINNING

'GEELONG VOLUNTEERS WELCOMED. DEMONSTRATION IN JOHNSTONE PARK'

After enlisting in October 1914, Herbert Roy Gollan went off to training camp and was among a group of Geelong volunteers who were given a civic send-off in Geelong's Johnstone Park on Tuesday December 15.

"Most of the Geelong men with the second Expeditionary Forces now in camp at Broadmeadows arrived here by train at 5 p.m. yesterday. They were on special leave, applied for by the Geelong citizens in order that they might tender them a suitable send-off. Altogether there were about 100 men. Geelong has a greater representation than that with the force, but a few of the men, owing to the hurried character of the arrangements, found themselves unable to come.

"There was an immense crowd in the vicinity of the railway station and along Malop and Moorabool streets. Much bunting was displayed. At the station the Mayor of Geelong formally welcomed the volunteers, and they then formed up and marched to Dickson's corner*. The general appearance and marching of the men was the subject of much favorable comment.

At 7.30 another procession, much larger and more imposing than the first, was formed at the corner of Moorabool and Myers Streets, and marched

---

*North-east corner of Moorabool and Ryrie Streets, occupied by T A Dickson, chemist.

to Johnstone Park... It was a fine show, and little wonder that a great crowd followed it into the park...

At half-past 9 the demonstration came to an end, and then the volunteers were entertained at supper in the ABC Cafe*. There were a few speeches. The mayor of Ceelong, on behalf of the Australian Natives Association, handed presents to volunteers HR Gollan, HE Hawkesworth, WJ Wray and AH Bowden. Another presentation was made by him on behalf of a friend to Mr W Beamond... and to Signaller B Asche.** All of the men will return to camp today."—Geelong Advertiser, December 16, 1914

* The ABC Cafe was in Moorabool Street opposite Little Malop Street.

**Roy Gollan was the only one of the first four men mentioned to return to Australia —

H E Hawksworth: Herbert Edwin Hawkesworth, a metallurgist, enlisted at the age of 33 and served at Gallipoli and in France. He sustained several wounds and while recovering in England died of the Spanish flu two weeks before the end of the war.

'WJ Wray': believed to be J W Rae – John William Rae. He worked as a driver and lived with his parents in East Geelong. He was killed in action at Gallipoli aged 22. About a year later his uncle, William Rae, who lived with the family in Geelong, died of wounds in France aged 45.

A H Bowden: Alfred Harlow Bowden was a young butcher living with his parents in East Geelong. He was killed in action at Pozieres in July 1916, a month before his 20th birthday.

The other two men who were presented with gifts —
W Beamond: William Robert Beamond was an 18-year-old grocery store employee at the time of enlistment. He progressed quickly through the ranks and returned to Australia a captain. He was Mentioned in Despatches during his service and was awarded the Military Cross. After his return he became a regional superintendant with the Shell company for many years.

B Asche: Herbert (Bert) George Asche lived with his father in Gheringhap Street. Prior to enlisting he had worked for a time at the billiard rooms of former Victorian billiards champion Tom Bragge in Moorabool Street. He returned safely to Australia.

ROY GOLLAN ~ LETTERS 1915-16

Letters from Egypt

'COMPETITIONS ON BOARD'
April 3, 1915
"Corporal HR GolIan, headquarters staff 3rd Light Horse, writes—
The geographical knowledge of the men came into question on the way over. An officer of high standing laid odds with another that there were not ten men in the rank and file who could name the capital of the United States. The test came. Men thought they were to be questioned re inoculation and were a bit nonplussed when faced with the question. School days were recalled by many, and the attempts at answers were some amusing and some ridiculous. New York was a hot favourite, but in the final was beaten by Winnipeg and Washington. Philadelphia and Ottawa were in the running but not placed. Another question was 'Who was the greatest general?' The layer of odds asserted that six men would name an Australian. Napoleon was declared the greatest general. Hannibal, Wellingon, Kitchener and French each had their supporters. General Booth was mentioned by four.

A SMART RASCAL
Life on board is pleasant enough. The absence of rough weather has not given rise to any incident. Men of all classes are congregated together; never was the quotation 'Son of a King, son of a Duke, son of a belted Earl' more aptly in evidence as the men gathered together, all going on the one mission.

Some there are who apply their cunning in the wrong direction. For example: When the boat was lying at Port Melbourne preparatory to leaving, no one was allowed to leave. One man however, contrived to see the last of his friends at close quarters. Cattle were being slung aboard in large boxes, and the last had been safely stowed in the stalls. The box this time, however, was not 'returned empty', for it contained our worthy friend who must have had a good shaking while in mid-air.

Once on the pier a transfer to the covered-in cattle waggon was easy, and he was driven out past the cordon of sentries without being detected. For this he was deprived leave at Fremantle, but managed to sneak ashore, hired a taxi, was driven into Perth and told the taxi driver he had been sent out on duty, and to collect the charge from the officer of the transport.

He evidently tired of a roaming life, and came and gave himself up on the next night, but was placed under arrest pending an enquiry.

He added further to his exploits on the day of sailing. Seeing a Press photographer on the wharf, he informed him that he was an aviator sent across from Melbourne to be specially attached to the WA Regiment. No doubt WA papers are now publishing a likeness of this great personage."

Letters from the Front

Lance-Sgt HR Gollan, Headquarters Staff, Mena Camp
April 9, 1915

"It was at midday on Saturday March 3 that we saw the first sign of movement. The tents of the Second Brigade, New South Wales Infantry, dropped, and the men prepared for the trek. Kits were packed and waggons loaded, and at dusk the brigade moved from the sand where they had done five months' solid training, onto the metal road, along which they swung with a light-hearted, glad-to-be-moving feeling that made us fellows who were destined to remain yet awhile, mad with envy.

The regimental bands seemed to catch the right notes with 'The Soldiers of the King' and other patriotic airs. The Light Horsemen just landed turned out to a man and lined the road, giving their comrades a rousing round of cheers as they departed. It was a great scene. Many were the hand-shakes exchanged as the column moved along and the

Mena military camp near Cairo, 1915.
It was here that the AIF trained prior to embarking for Gallipoli.

"Good-byes" and "good lucks" proffered. Not a downcast man amongst the lot. Sing, well they kept up their reputation for that when "march at ease" was given. 'Tipperary' seems to have died a natural death, and something more original superseded it:

> Marching, marching, marching,
> Always jolly well marching,
> When we're dead and in our graves,
> Our marching will be done.

It was a never-to-be-forgotten experience, and probably we shall be in their place in a few months, being farewelled by a future Australian contingent. I am in the best of health. Now that the First Australian Division has gone, I have taken charge of the post office at Mena Camp, having several assistants, which means a lot of work, especially when we strike an Australian and English mail the same week."

About the same time Roy Gollan's letter from Egypt is published in the 'Advertiser', another letter, written by Lieut Dickson*, describes events on the European front.

April 3, 1915

"I write this from the actual fire trench at 2.15pm on Easter Saturday. The Bosches are about 18 yards away and this afternoon rather quiet. Our artillery rattled them a little this morning. We are in rather an extraordinary trench, on the edge of part of a turnip field. It has been impossible to dig far down owing to the number of Frenchmen buried in these parts....

Yesterday was rather nice, the sun was shining and but for a little shelling in the afternoon, things were quiet. Our aeroplane made a prolonged reconnaissance of their lines, and they poofed at them with their anti-aircraft guns, which are not good.

In the evening, I went out with a large party to improve our defence lines. We were out for about three hours right in the open. Their star shells light up the whole of the countryside; they then fire rapidly if they see anything which rouses their suspicions. The chances are dead against one being hit by an aimed shot. The danger is from a chance stray bullet—of course that is where the luck of the game comes in. However, it is very uncanny out there so close to their lines. We had a shower of rain which did not make matters more comfortable.

There was more rain this morning and this makes things very sticky and uncomfortable. The worst of this trench is that there is nasty crossfire. They have a point of advantage on our left flank which enables them to drop an occasional bullet into the trench. During the day rifle fire is spasmodic. It is about dusk that things liven up. We go back to the supports tonight for two days and then come here again for two more days."

April 4, 1915

"I am writing this by the light of the lantern dimly burning in a little Belgian farmhouse. We came back here last night from the fire trench. I am here with my command and occupy an apartment which I haven't *[established]* yet to be a pig-sty or the cowshed; certain I am that it is either one or the other. On the floor there is straw, and the roof is of straw."

*Believed to be from Lt W Everard Dickson, son of Moorabool Street chemist TA Dickson.
 Everard Dickson became a barrister in London and later became the first Australian to hold a London magistracy.

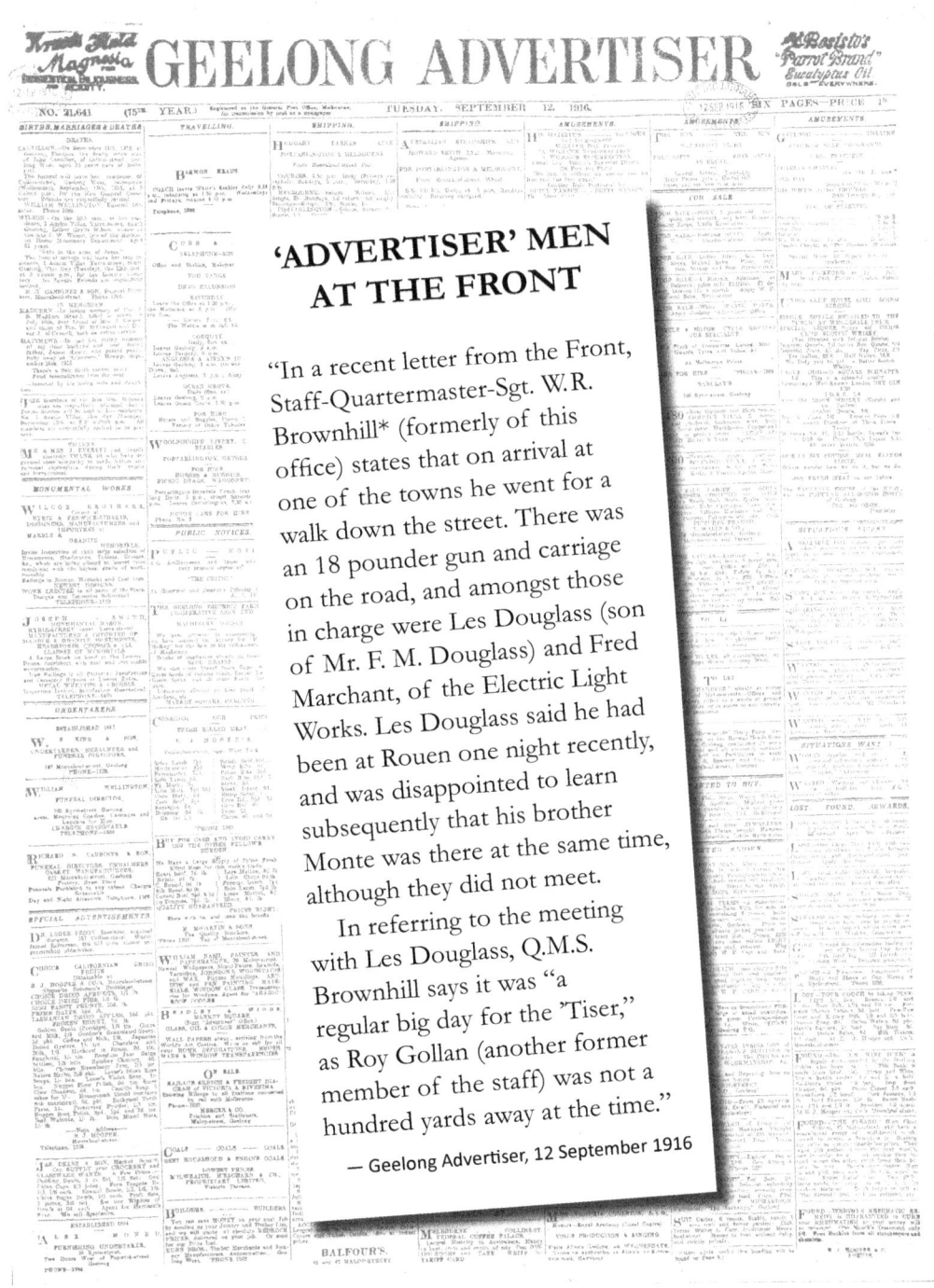

'ADVERTISER' MEN AT THE FRONT

"In a recent letter from the Front, Staff-Quartermaster-Sgt. W.R. Brownhill* (formerly of this office) states that on arrival at one of the towns he went for a walk down the street. There was an 18 pounder gun and carriage on the road, and amongst those in charge were Les Douglass (son of Mr. F. M. Douglass) and Fred Marchant, of the Electric Light Works. Les Douglass said he had been at Rouen one night recently, and was disappointed to learn subsequently that his brother Monte was there at the same time, although they did not meet.

In referring to the meeting with Les Douglass, Q.M.S. Brownhill says it was "a regular big day for the 'Tiser," as Roy Gollan (another former member of the staff) was not a hundred yards away at the time."

— Geelong Advertiser, 12 September 1916

*Walter Randolph Brownhill would later write the definitive history of Geelong with 'The History of Geelong and Corio Bay', 1955.

'GEELONG MEN IN FIRING LINE'

(published August 26, 1915)

From Sgt Major H R Gollan (late of The 'Advertiser' Staff)

'GABA TEPE LIKE BARWON HEADS'

On service, June 24, 1915

"Passing along the trenches the other day it gave me quite a pleasant sensation to see the familiar cover of the 'News of the Week,' and a few minutes conversation with the owner soon persuaded him to lend me the edition. It was a treat to read of the stirring recruiting meeting you had in the theatre, and I sincerely hope that the young fellows will rally to the call and come to our assistance. I often think of my own experiences in Geelong and the happy times spent, and therefore like to keep up my old associations by letting you know how Geelong boys are doing over here on the shores of T-----.

Imagine a place like the Bluff at Barwon Heads, only three times the height, and extending four to five miles along the coast. Imagine this and you have a good conception of the position now occupied by the Australians and New Zealanders.

Truly, it was a wonderful achievement to take it as they did, and the rows of silent graves along the beach speak in pathetic tones of one of the heroic events of this terrible struggle. What a change at this spot now to the night of the memorable April 25th.

A pier juts out into the Aegean Sea, and destroyers land their cargoes of ammunition and stores almost directly onto the backs of the mules, who do the transport to the trenches. The hills have transformed into miniature towns and villages — or the whole position might be likened to a city — ANZAC (Australian and New Zealand Army Corps) Cove being the city proper, with suburbs styled Monash Gully, Walker's Ridge, Quinn's Post and a host of others. The whole is a scene of great activity, for no sooner has a man done his term in the trenches than he is taken off to the base to assist in the handling and the transport of the munitions of war.

Sandbagged troops at Gallipoli

Charles Bean stands in the long communications sap (trench) at Gallipoli that ran from the Anzac position through to the New Zealand headquarters; it was 2.4m deep and wide enough for two donkeys to pass through.
Picture: Philip Schuler

Courtesy Australian War Memorial

Trenches have to be continually improved and communications saps [trenches] cut. One moves in a continuous maze of saps and trenches, but soon becomes acquainted with regular routes to places such as Shrapnel Gully......."

[1] Captain Joseph Terrell ('Tyrrell') Crowl, Dalgetys auctioneer, was the first officer from Geelong to be killed in the war.

Crowl, a tall, natural sportsman, played several seasons for the Chilwell football team and a few games for Geelong Football Club in 1906. He died on 27 June 1915, aged 30. A photo of his grave in Ari Burnu Cemetery, Gallipoli, was sent home by fellow Geelong soldier JSR (Sam) Heath.

Pte AM Douglass to his parents Mr and Mrs FM Douglass.
Tuesday June 26, 1915

"We are still in the firing line. Yesterday we had several fireworks displays trying to draw the Turk. They landed one of their "John Jacksons" into one of the observation posts. It made a great mess, but otherwise did very little damage. Poor Tyrrell Crowl[1] was killed on Sunday while out in the trenches resting.

This morning we had quite a swagger breakfast — bacon and eggs, fresh bread and jam and tea. Bacon, jam and cheese are a daily ration, with a tin of tea for each meal and a pound and a quarter of fresh bread every second day, and fresh meat every now and again. For tea, which is hot, we alternate stew and vegetables or bully beef and hot mashed potatoes and boiled onions mixed together, so really we do not fare too badly. Our weekly tobacco issue averages about two packets of cigarettes and an ounce of tobacco, with one box of matches per man. This morning we were presented with a cover for our caps as shade for our necks. The caps, which have linoleum lining, have been terribly hot. Why our felt hats were taken away from us will ever remain unknown — like a good many other things…"

Roy Gollan writes to his parents from Gallipoli, dated October 15, 1915

"...I will now give you a short history of our leaving since our first baptism of fire. On the ---- of August we received money that was owing to us and were told to buy cigarettes or other likely things, as it was expected that we would be at the front within a week. Our hearts were going a bit for a few seconds, and then we ---- with joy after eleven months in Egypt, marching and blowing away sands..."

Gollan was aboard one of the transport ships carrying troops for Gallipoli on September 2, 1915, when one, HMT Southland, was torpedoed by a German submarine in the Aegean Sea. His letter continues:

"... missed us by about 10 feet. Most of the chaps from the Southland seemed happy enough on the rafts and boats etc. They were singing 'This Is The Life' and other bits of songs and some with their feet dangling in the water, saying they had "cold feet". But when we got them on board they nearly all fainted and broke down; some of them were in a pretty bad mess—hands cut to pieces from the ropes, others with nasty cuts from the falling of things when the torpedo struck. We did not mess about long, as it was too dangerous. We set off for Lemnos, which we reached at 5 o'clock the same night. Before we left the Southland there were 21 boats in sight coming to assist. What do you think of that for wireless?

We stopped on Lemnos just on two days. I had some lovely swims whilst there. It is a bonzer harbour, not unlike Geelong, better and deeper, but not quite as big. The place is just crammed with boats, warships, etc.

On Saturday 4th September, at 1 o'clock, we boarded a smaller boat in the charge of naval officers, and at 4 p.m. we left for the scene of fighting. We got there about 9.30 p.m. and did not get ashore till 1 on the Sunday morning. It was very funny whilst waiting to get into the smaller boats to land, the warships were bombarding along the coast and stray bullets were flying everywhere; it was pitch dark, we of course thought they were all meant for us, and were having some jokes about it; none of our chaps were hit anyhow. When we got into the smaller boats to go ashore, it was a very rough sea and it was darned uncomfortable. There was about 100 in our boat, and they were nearly all sick. We got ashore safely—and with pack and ammunition, three days' tucker and God knows what, it was equal to about 1cwt [about 50kg]. I reckon we sneaked inland about half a mile up hill and down gully. I was that knocked up that I just fell down where we had to camp and went to sleep and didn't care if all the Turks in the world came along. I did not sleep too well on account of the row.

When day broke we made a bit of breakfast and then started exploring.

On Monday we took our position and have been doing well since. I was not too bad under fire for the first time; it seems natural after our training; but as far as getting used to it, the big guns, etc, it's impossible. No one ever will, but there is only one gun, or battery of guns, I should say, that we are all really nervous of. It is the 75s. They are French guns, but the Turks have got them. You know what my job of stretcher bearer must be like when we see the wounded arriving..."

"... a nice trip to Cairo. I knew two of the sisters on the train and was well looked after. First we got a packet of British Red Cross stuff; cigarettes, handkerchiefs, soap, paper and envelopes, then later we got chocolate, biscuits, cocoa, beef tea, lemon drinks etc. and more cigarettes from the old Indian doctor with many ribbons on his breast who was on the train when I had dealings last August.

Got to Cairo at midday and were whisked away in motor ambulances to Ghezireh, which was a magnificent hotel on the banks of one branch of the Nile and is perhaps the best hospital to be in, in Egypt. It has just been made exclusively Australian. All the doctors, nurses and orderlies are Australians and they are all very good sports.

The doctors at Anzac were afraid I had contracted enteric fever [typhoid], as my temperature was consistently high for some weeks, but then as it didn't develop,

The Ghezireh Palace Hotel became Australian General Hospital No 2 and was Roy Gollan's first convalescent stop.

they came to the conclusion that the inoculation (which was done twice, once at Broadmeadows, and again in Egypt) had saved me. Dr E. Cordner* (Captain) sent me away for a time, and now our doctor here in the convalescent ward is Captain Bennie (Dr B. of Armidale) and he is kind-hearted and considerate to a degree. The first morning when he had written out my report, he said that as soon as I was better, I should get into the Dental Corps, as I was doubly eligible, and men were badly needed on it. (Cable since received says 'Dental address, Helonan,' that place being a town some miles up on the hill, and connected with Cairo by electric tram, and where there is a large camp of convalescents.) The doctor said that I was very much run down at present. I can only just manage to walk round.

There are three of us in a fine third-storey room, with a magnificent view of gardens, the Nile palms and fine buildings. At first I was not confined to bed, but now have been for three days on account of weakness, but today I am up for a while, and feel that I will soon regain my strength and weight, due to the good care we are getting here. The food is good. I get chicken, fish, eggs, broth, pudding, custard etc. and a bottle of stout every day—all very decent.

There is a large library in the building. I don't know how long I will be here in this hospital. We may get moved to another or to a rest camp, but I expect to be under the good treatment here for at least a fortnight, and don't expect to go back to the front (if I have to) for some time yet, so don't worry about me at all, for I am doing excellently, and am in a good position to recover myself well."

Latest News from JSR *[John Samuel Robert (Sam)]* Heath
October 27, 1915

"Gallipoli, Anzac Cove.—Things are getting steadily colder now. We have to go 48 hours on stretcher-bearing up the hill now, and 24 hours off (some of that pick and shovel) and the latest is that after seven weeks fixing dugouts and levelling off for a number of hospital tents and getting settled down, we have to move camp... It's a bit hard... I put in a whole day putting a stove and fireplace into our dugout. I made the stove with a kerosene tin with a grate in it...and a chimney made of the four sides of a

---

*Dr Edward (Ted) Cordner of Melbourne. Cordner was also a VFL player in early 1900s.

biscuit tin rolled out lengthwise. It occasionally smokes us out but it's very nice having cafe-au-lait and toast and jam for supper."

Staff Sergeant Roy Gollan is ill with enteric fever and is transferred to No 3 Western General Hospital at Cardiff. He writes to his mother at the family home in Elizabeth Street, Geelong West.

October 31, 1915

"I tried hard in Malta to get back to the Peninsula, but the doctors, after consultation, decided that it would be better to send me to England to get a thorough bracing up first. Perhaps they were right. There is certainly less danger of a relapse here, and the change of scenery will do me wonders.

We left Malta a week ago on a fine hospital ship and landed at Southampton yesterday, and were conveyed to Cardiff Hospital in a splendid hospital train.

When at Malta we were treated splendidly, and it is the same here, and it was a treat to meet and talk with nice kind-hearted women-folk again. And the gifts they brought us, too! The Australians are tremendously popular. There are 12 Australians and one New Zealander in the hospital now. Very few of the latter are left. The war seems to have come home very close to the people here, and there were some sad hearts amongst those who came to see us yesterday.

In the evening at 6 o'clock the minister and choir of a neighbourhood church held a service prior to going to their own church. It was a treat to join in a good sing again, and my word, those Welsh people can sing!

Picture 2014
Cardiff's Royal Infirmary housed Australia's Western General Hospital No 3, where Roy Gollan spent further time.

The chat to the men was soul-inspiring, for at the church afterwards they were to have a memorial service to several of the young men of the choir who had fallen in France.

We expect to be sent to a convalescent home in a few days, but may not remain there long. I am feeling quite strong again, and will soon be my usual self. I think there was some good purpose in my coming here as at the close of the war only a few Australians will come over here. I may count myself lucky in getting here now, and missing the dreaded winter on the Peninsula."

Excerpt from an unnamed soldier's letter, published the same day:

"...We are still in rest camp and having a good time. We often play football against the navy who are a fine lot of sports.

One of the battleships brought their band over recently and gave us a ripping concert. They had some great comics among them. I enjoyed it better than any concert I ever saw. These naval chaps are marvels; they carry on just as if there was no war, and behind it is that determined look which makes them born of the seas. I don't think half the people realise what we owe to them jolly Tars. Thanks for the 'News of the Week'; it is all right to get a bit of news from home."

In November, Roy writes to his father from Peterley Farm, Great Missenden, Buckinghamshire, England

November 7, 1915

"I have been sent here to convalesce, away from the rush and tear of a big city, and to be free from the rigors and discipline of a military hospital. People are most anxious to get a colonial into their home, and so I find myself sent to the home of Mr and Mrs Greaves at the above address—a real old country home with plenty of beautiful ground, plenty of fine horses and all the other incidentals of a good old English home. I have only been here one day, having arrived last night, and already feel at home and am looking forward to a bracing fortnight amongst the hills and the horses. You have no idea of the beauty of the English scenery until you have seen the autumn tints in all their glory.

Since last I wrote you will observe that I have left Cardiff and have been to that wonderful city—London. We (that is, about six Australians from Cardiff) went up three days ago and reported to the Australian Military Headquarters, where we were examined by a Medical Board. Two were sent to a convalescent camp, and the remainder, including myself, was ordered to leave the city.

On Thursday morning, Sgt Doreen and I went to Buckingham Palace at 10.30 to see the guard change — a beautiful and historic sight in peace time, when the soldiers wear their gorgeous uniforms, but war has shorn all the pomp, or much of it, away, and now the Grenadier Guards are dressed in the universal khaki.

Strictly at 10.30 the old guard parades in front of the palace, and a few minutes later the new guard comes marching along, headed by the famous Grenadier Guards Band in their big busbies* and long, dark overcoats. The band falls in behind the new guard, the drums and fife by their side, and to the strain of an imposing, slow ceremonial march, the old guard is met by the new. Presentation of arms takes place, the officer of the old guard hands over the keys of the colours to the officer of the new guard, and then the relief of the sentries round the Palace takes place. While this is going on, the band plays for half an hour underneath the King's window. The band then marches the old guard back to Chelsea Barracks. So taken were the sergeant and I with the playing of the band that we followed them to the barracks, and did not realise the distance until we had to trudge back. In the afternoon we paid a visit to the National Art Gallery and saw a recruitment meeting in Trafalgar Square. You have no idea of the tremendous traffic about the Square.

Next morning we visited the War Office and Admiralty Office. We saw the Royal Life Guards in their beautiful bright red jackets and a number of guns which were captured from the Germans. That night both of us were invited to spend the evening with Mr and Mrs Deakin**, and had a most enjoyable time. Of course after dinner they wanted us to relate our experiences to their interested circle of friends and posed questions. People have a high admiration for the struggle for the Dardanelles which is considered as being more serious than France. As I look back on my months there, I just marvel that I got off with nothing worse than I am now recovering from. About 8000 Australians are in England and a great number are going back to the same company. I have to go before a board at the end of my furlough and am certain of rejoining my brigade. My ---- did not like to be sent back. There is a rumour that our ---- got our horses.

*Headdresses
**Former prime minister Alfred Deakin was in London with his wife to consult medical specialists.

I went to church at Missenden with Mr and Mrs Greaves. It's an English church with a long history. I intend after a fortnight to visit those relatives of ours in Scotland and may put in a fortnight amongst them. I am feeling quite fit again and suppose I'll be sent back. I saw a funny thing the other day. It depicted a Turk howling in pain, and saying—'I've taken some Turkish delight and it's getting into my Dardanelles.' *[This may have been a reference to diarrhoea, or an STD. It happened to thousands of soldiers.]* There are not many who can say they were there four and a half months. I am going to London tomorrow to see the Mayor's procession and return at night. We are only a few miles from London."

Extracts from letter from Sergeant Louis Dardel, 13th Light Horse December 11, 1915

"Mails have been very scarce here lately, but I went to see [brother] Eric the other day and found him in the middle of his mail, and so I had a good read of his letters. We usually work this business on the co-operative lines. When Sergt Hollis came back from ---- the other day, I was in the trenches, so he sent me up a little light luncheon.

On many occasions a big camp like this sounds like a big bee-hive at night, but on Christmas Eve those who were not singing were playing some more or less weird instrument, seemingly designed with the one object of making a row. Talk of 'sounds of revelry at night'.

My billy was from Mavis Bell of the Presbyterian Ladies College. We got quite a number from there, and I saw to it that I got one from that lot. And it was a jolly fine billy,

Picture: Australian War Memorial

Soldiers display their Christmas billies. The gift billies, filled with treats from home, were extremely popular with the troops.

and in it was the best letter that I've had for a long time (considering that I've not had any for two months). The billies were a great idea and I just wish you could have seen the boys with them. One of our fellows got one from two little girls of eight from the Presbyterian Ladies College. It was packed mainly with toys and I think it caused as much merriment as any other. We also got Christmas Puddings, one per two men, and they were splendid. I got one from the Stawell Red Cross Society, so I must send them a line. Eric is camped just over the way and I've seen Douglas and Les Hawkins since I came here. Les looks well and is a fine type of Australian."

From Pte Clive Newman*
At sea. Saturday December 25

Dear Family, the Peninsula is finished, so far as the Australians were concerned. The embarkation orders came very suddenly. Am meeting old friends every hour. Not allowed to tell you their units. Austin (GS) looks very well. We left very early on Friday morning and have been going as fast as the boat can be driven. Submarines are the danger we are looking for. Everyone has to wear a life belt all day, and use it for a pillow at night. In addition, there are guards posted all round the ship to look out for one of the cursed things. I am one of the corporals on the present submarine guard, an easy job, but I will be darned glad to get on land again. When a man is anticipating a watery grave every minute, a sea trip has its disadvantages. And today is Christmas Day, heigh-ho. Suppose you have all finished an excellent dinner and feeling at peace with the world. Well, just let me tell you what we had. For breakfast, as much porridge as would fill an egg-cup. Then bread and butter. For dinner, meat and bread, soup, and for tea we will get bread with no jam or butter, and so there you are, but a man shall not growl, he is lucky to be alive and well enough to eat.

I hear that several boats have been sunk with mail on board.

Heliopolis, December 29, 1915

Got here Monday. Did not sight any submarines on the way across. We are getting on the horses right away. Won't be long before we are back again, this time on horseback. We got a big mail today, the first in three months. About six letters, one from Dot and some cash from the mater..."

*Clive F Newman was a great-uncle of later Geelong footballer and media identity Sam Newman.

From Staff-Sergeant JSR Heath[2]
Dental Staff, Helonan Convalescent Home for Australians and New Zealanders, Cairo

Boxing Day, 1915

"Christmas Day has come and gone, but I got the best Christmas gift I could have wished for—that is, about 40 back letters with all the welcome news. Christmas Day was very decent here—palm leaves and other decorations all over the place. There was a good dinner of turkey and plum pudding. Got a small tea tin of Red Cross Gifts. I tell you everyone highly appreciated these; they were very good indeed.

I'm glad you got the cables. It was difficult getting them away from the Peninsula. One day when we were over there, a fellow was brought out of the trenches to us. He had his hat over his face so that we couldn't see who he was, and when we got him down to the ambulance, who should it be but Bryant Mills, who had been taken suddenly with cramps. They say here that Monte Douglass[3] was a hero, doing brave things over and over again.

I am sending you some photos I took of incidents in connection with the torpedoing of the transport Southland when we were going across in September last. The one showing some of the survivors in a crowded boat singing 'Here We Are Again' as we came up to them, is good. Thanks awfully for the parcels; they are coming to hand now. I believe they didn't send any to the Dardanelles for some time before the evacuation. Those who were at Gallipoli are now Mediterranean Expeditionary Force.

We are very busy here and there is plenty to do. I have to give my whole time and attention to it. I see that some

[2] Born in Geelong in 1893, JSR Heath had partly trained as a dentist when he enlisted in the medical corps. He served at Gallipoli (Mentioned in Dispatches for bravery) and later in France. He resumed his dental training after the war and in his later career, was the first private Australian to own an X-ray machine and, say descendants, up-ended the old-school dental establishment.

[3] Monte Douglass (1888-1957) was a journalist whose family had owned the 'Geelong Advertiser' since 1864. Among his mates at the front, Douglass was known as the 'Water Carrier' — whenever water was wanted in the firing line, it was always Douglass who volunteered to go for it, "and over a bullet-swept area he walked as calmly as if he was crossing Moorabool Street," wrote a friend.

of our chaps are getting six months' furlough with an extra allowance, a few of them are leaving here today.... Please thank all known and unknown friends who sent me Christmas greetings and as you see, I got most of them on Christmas Eve. So that was just the thing. Tell the boys that when in the hospital I got fed up on oranges and dried figs from the Grecian archipelago. Each fig had about three grubs in it, but then — well, I believe in a meat diet."

AUSTRALIAN WAR MEMORIAL

Rescuers come alongside a crowded boatload of HMT Southland survivors, September 2, 1915, as described by Sgt Heath.

Driver Leslie Frederick Douglass [brother of Monte Douglass]
To his parents from No 4 Auxiliary Hospital, Egypt

December 27, 1915

"We have arrived safely in Egypt and outside Cairo it is a barren-looking spot. We landed at Suez and came on by train to Zeitoun, where we detrained and marched out to the Aerodrome camp at Heliopolis. Since arriving I have been unfortunate enough to contract measles, and I was shifted down to Abbassia, where all the infectious cases are dealt with. Keith Urquhart* is also here, which makes it better as we have to put in three or four weeks.

An aeroplane flew right over the hospital this morning, so Keith and I hopped out of bed to see it, as we had not seen one before.... I managed to get into Cairo one night before I got ill, Keith Howe** and I went in together. We started by having a good square meal at a French cafe called Soult, and afterwards walked round the city, to see what we could.... I had a chat with several educated Egyptians who seemed quite decent sort of chaps, but I should think one would require to be very careful what he says in Cairo, as there are many spies knocking round. We get a half-holiday on Saturday and Sunday, and 25 per cent are allowed leave into Cairo every night.

Keith Urquhart and I got out of bed yesterday for the first time, and have enjoyed ourselves sitting on the wall which surrounds the hospital, watching the traffic go past between here and Cairo. I am longing to get some letters as we have not had a mail yet. All is well with me."

---

*Arthur Keith Urquhart was a 24-year-old grazier who had attended Geelong Grammar. He and his brother Rod survived Gallipoli (though Keith was wounded), but Rod was killed in action later in Egypt. In a further loss, Keith's father died at their station, 'Boonerah' at Hexham, in 1917 before Keith returned home.

**Keith Thomas Howe, grazier and another former Geelong Grammar compatriot of Douglass's. He sustained gunshot wounds to upper body and leg. He and Douglass returned home on the same ship after the war.

From Sgt James Alexander (Alex) Reid*, to his parents in Malop Street

Late December 1915

"The censorship has become very strict, so I am not able to tell you as much as I would like. Last year at Christmas we slept on the sand of Barwon Heads, this year on the sands of the desert. We have plenty of interesting work to do, and it is a great honour for our battalion to be picked for active service so soon. We are in the most important post in the -----. I was out all night on outpost duty, and today, though being pretty tired, we had a good time, and I can say we had a great feed, Christmas puddings from West Australia, one pudding between two of us. One of the boys had a box with cakes, etc. sent to him, so with oranges and tomatoes we had a jolly good time. The chocolate and toffee you gave me when I left I am keeping for a rainy day.

Am sorry we didn't stay in Heliopolis a little longer; but we had orders to move off at a minute's notice. We left at 10 o'clock on Monday night, and arrived at 3 o'clock at ----- on the Canal and slept in the train until daylight. Then we moved on to -----. A little later we went on board barges and were towed to where we are at present, and relieved a fine body of troops. The Turks have a railway built within 20 miles of where we are. It is a bonzer place and we are having a fine time, though plenty of guard work and in our spare time we have good sport, swimming and fishing in the Canal. -------"

From Staff-Sergeant H R Gollan, c/- Australian Military Offices, 130 Horseferry Road, Westminster

December 29, 1915

"No doubt you have heard of my being invalided to England—thoroughly knocked out and exhausted after five months on that terrible peninsula. I smile at times now when I think of me, who thought I was so strong, laid low in hospital for two months.

Truly, I was lucky to remain in that death-trap at Gallipoli for so long without injury. But I am myself once again, and leave in a few days time to rejoin and assist in the reorganisation of the brigade in Egypt. I still hold the rank of brigade staff sergeant

---

* Alex Reid, a Malop Street butcher, was killed in action the following year, in July 1916.

to the 3rd Light Horse, but hope for promotion before long. I could get transferred to the British Army if I wish, but prefer to remain with Australia. All the original brigade staff are out of action now. I met Mr Monte Douglass last week at the London HQ. He is looking well and has got a commission in the RFA (British Army) and goes into training in Glasgow. Young [Albert] Anderson, who was in the Geelong Light Horse, is also convalescing here. RSM [Charles] Lucas (late of 20th LH Geelong, but now Lieut 4th LH) hopes to return to his regiment with the next draft. I got the greatest surprise the other day to meet Tom Sutterby in London[4]. He had not enlisted when I left. He looks well now, but a Medical Board will decide his future destinies.

Probably you remember Parrington[5] of 'Country Girl' and Ford car fame. He now holds a position in the records office on the London Staff. Lieut-Col. [Arthur] Deeble hopes to soon take over once again command of the gallant 8th LH who suffered so severely in the charge by our brigade at the Nek, Walkers' Ridge, on August 7th.

As you will probably have guessed, Fleet Street has been a great rendez-vous of mine whilst in London. I have met numbers of pressmen of all grades, and in comparing their conditions with ours, give me Australia every time. I have received a number of introductions through Mr Gough, manager of the London office of the 'Argus'. Mr Murdoch[6], of the Sydney 'Sun' and Melbourne 'Herald', invited me to dine with him and I have lent him my diary, and gave facts and figures of Gallipoli which he incorporated in the 'Times History of the War', the Dardanelles portion of which he is writing.

Don't worry over me, we are all as happy as the day is long and only waiting for the Turks to come along. Hope the

[4] Tom Sutterby, one of Geelong's leading amateur entertainers, was badly injured in an ankle and was kept on administrative duties for the remainder of the war. He performed with 'The Anzac Coves' on a tour of France in 1919, and returned to a theatrical career in Australia.

[5] Henry Beaumont Parrington was a partner in a Kardinia Street garage and Ford agency. He is mentioned in this letter for his appearance in a musical comedy, 'A Country Girl', in Geelong in 1913. Parrington returned home safely.

[6] Keith Murdoch, reporter and founder of the News Ltd media empire, and father of Rupert Murdoch.

boys are enlisting well; they are all wanted over here.

It was through Mr *[Thomas]* Naylor of the 'Daily Chronicle' that I got into the Press Gallery at the House of Commons, and I have several times been in the Public Gallery. Mr Asquith, Mr Lloyd-George and Sir Edward Grey are all worth hearing, and their utterances will have an additional interest once having seen them in the place where the great Empire is governed. When in Edinburgh I was fortunate in having a thorough look at the office of the 'Scotsman', and meeting the staff. Truly, this establishment is run on the latest devices which would take a fair-sized book to explain. I dined with the proprietor* in the evening. Strange to say, his daughter married one of the Mackinnons of the 'Argus'. I met the staffs of both Aberdeen papers and compared experiences. Quite a number of them are in khaki, and some have even given their lives."

Roy Gollan

'NURSES RETURN THANKS TO GEELONG'
February 17, 1916

'Red Cross Nurses return thanks to Geelong'

"The Geelong and District War Funds secretary has received this letter from nurses at the front—

'May I ... acknowledge your Christmas Box to me at AGH No 2 in Egypt? It would be difficult to express the pleasure it gave me to receive the box of good things your society enclosed. All were in perfect order and everything most acceptable. I am, I know, only trying to express what all the nurses feel; it was like the excitement of Christmas Day in our own country when each fresh article was unpacked.

Yours etc.

Winifred Hay.'

1st Australian Military Hospital, Harefield Park, London
December 25, 1915

'It gives me much pleasure to acknowledge your splendid Xmas box received by me on Christmas Eve. If you could only have witnessed our pleasure and delight on receiving and unpacking same, you would all have felt fully repaid for all the time and expense

---

*Referring to James Law, general manager of 'The Scotsman'. His daughter Hilda Law married Lauchlan Mackinnon, whose family owned the Melbourne 'Argus'.

spent on us. We were indeed a very happy and jolly party of nurses, and were just as excited as children. The boxes are simply beautiful and contain such a variety of useful and nice things. We all think they were wonderfully packed, and appreciate every article.

I will tell you what was in my box — 3 handkerchiefs, 1 pair warm stockings, 1 bottle eau de cologne, 2 cakes soap, 1 box violet powder, 1 box boracic powder, 4 packets of hairpins, 1 tin shortbread,1 tin biscuits, 1 packet notepaper, 2 pkts post cards, 1 bottle smelling salts, 1 bottle of iodine and brush, 1 tin Cadbury's chocolates, 1 sweet little Red Cross. Will you and your helpers accept my best thanks for your more than handsome gift? I am a Victorian, and feel proud to be one. The misses McKenzie, of 'Riviera' and 'Bellaria', of Geelong are personal friends of mine and I am quite glad my box came from a town where I know someone.

"Our Boys" at Harefield Park had a very nice Christmas and all enjoyed themselves. There were competitions for best decorated wards, and all entered into it with great enthusiasm. Xmas trees, Xmas boxes, and splendid Xmas dinner, helped make things merry and bright and everything passed off without a hitch. Our boys gave the children of Harefield Village a Christmas tea and tree, and you can imagine the delight of the little ones. There is a rumour that the name of the village is to be changed to Austral Town.

Yours etc.　　　　　　　　　　　　　　　　　　　　　　　　　　　　　　Eveline Nicholson.'

Heliopolis, Egypt. 1st Australian Gen. Hospital
December 25, 1915

Nurse Alice Grace Douglas

'Among my pretty and useful articles in my box sent by the subscribers to Lady Bridges' appeal, was a card from the residents of Geelong and district. My home has been in Geelong for many years, though my work lay in Melbourne. It was therefore specially pleasing to me to receive a direct greeting from the city. Very many thanks. We have all derived much delight from the contents of the thoughtfully and kindly packed boxes. The patients all appeared to spend a very happy Christmas day, in which decorations, concerts, gifts, extra good fare, cigars and billies, contributed.

Yours etc,　　　　　　　　　　　　　　　　　　　　　　　　　　　　　　Grace Douglas.'

HS Neuralia, Liverpool, December 29, 1915

"Thank you very much indeed for the most delightful and useful lot of presents from you in the Christmas parcel received today. Five of we Australian girls are on the above ship and although we have had in some ways a very happy Christmas, have felt it very much having no remembrances from home or the dear homeland. Being on transport work, our mails are very irregular, and we probably will not receive our Christmas letters until February, making it about three months since we had our last home mails.

Had you seen us all opening our various parcels, like so many children with their Christmas stockings, you would have realised our appreciation; it is greater than a child's for we realise the thoughts and kindness contained in such a hamper. We have been working on the Dardanelles transport since the beginning of engagements in April, so we have seen a great deal of our own as well as other wounded men. Ours was the ship to go to the rescue of the Southland which contained the 21st and I think 23rd Divisions (Victorian).

I send you in case anyone might care for it, a snap, as we viewed her as we drew near.

Yours etc

Sister DD *[Daisy]* Richmond."

Harefield Park House, London. Picture shows rear of house and lake. The property, offered by an Australian couple resident in England, became No1 Australian Auxiliary Hospital. It was the only purely Australian hospital in England.

Erected 1920
by Mustafa Kemal Attaturk

Photograph by Wendy Hebbard, 2001

Respect to the Mehmetçik Memorial, Anzac Cove, Gallipoli Peninsula.

The monument depicts a Turkish soldier carrying a wounded Australian officer, and is based on an actual event. An inscription attributed to Ataturk speaks in part to 'you the mothers of the Johnnies and Mehmets' whose sons lie peacefully beneath the soil, 'wipe away your tears; after having lost their lives on this land they have become our sons as well.'

Mehmetçik is a term used to affectionately refer to soldiers of the Turkish army, akin to 'Diggers' in Australia.

Photograph by Wendy Hebbard, 2001

Anzac Cove

More from Roy Gollan
(undated, published in the 'Advertiser' February 17, 1916)

"Had they chosen, every man from Anzac convalescing in England could have had three Christmas Dinners on Xmas day, and there would still have remained numbers of unaccepted invitations. This was one of England's ways of expressing sympathy with the hard luck which has marked the conclusion of the first great essay made by Australia in the War. One day after the official announcement of the withdrawal from Anzac, the tide of hospitable invitations from English people to men of the Australian force, already a very respectable stream, had swollen to the proportions of a flood. Hostesses who had made preparations for a Christmas treat found too late that there were no guests available, so rather than allow the preparations to go for nought, men from the hospitals were asked to partake. Truly, there was not a lonely soldier in London at Xmas.

It would be hard to describe the feelings of Australians when news of the evacuation of Anzac was first published. Feelings of relief mixed with feelings of regret; experiences of those weary months in the trenches retained; and wonderings how those at home would receive the news. But next day came Mr Fisher's assurance that "the evacuation would serve but as a spur to further effort to see the conflict through to a satisfactory conclusion." Then the infantrymen stepped out with a firmer step, despite fever weakness, and the light horseman slapped his riding whip against his legging—glad at the prospect at being mounted once more.

"These wounded Australians are the best immigration agents Australia could have"—so remarked a Londoner, and he is not far wrong. Travel where you will—England, Ireland, Scotland, Wales—there you will see the light brown khaki and the saucy wide-awake hat. These lads can be relied upon to talk about Australia and its prospects. Their fine physique, which is the admiration of all, is an advertisement in itself. Many an English lad who has spent his life in factory or office and has tasted the free open life in the army, will, when peace once more reigns, turn his steps to our open plains. Many have already expressed their intention of doing so. And they will not be strangers when they land in the new country. They will be met by friends alongside whom they fought on the memorable day of the Suvla Bay landing, or who, perhaps, were ward-mates in hospital.

Strengthening the bond between the Colonies and the Mother Country is taking place every day by the relationships existing between Australian wounded and their English friends. Relatives have been found in curious ways. Our forefathers who pictured Australia neglected correspondence which would have established the connecting link; with the result that all trace of English ancestors was lost. Now comes the Australian to trace them out. Here is a case in point—A young Light Horseman is discharged from hospital. He knows he has relatives in Scotland, but knows nothing of their whereabouts except the country or shire in which, perhaps, his grandfather lived before migrating. The young Australian takes a ticket to the largest town *[this young Australian was possibly Roy himself. Bert also looked up some relatives in Scotland]* in that shire away in the north of Scotland, and on arrival consults the local directory, finds the name and makes himself known. One can easily picture the surprise when once his identity is established.

The arrival of the Australian into the northern country town causes not a little interest amongst the townsfolk. Two small boys were heard conjecturing as to the nationality of one of our boys—"He's an officer of the Boy Scouts," said the first. "Garn wid ye," said number two. "Yon is an Australian; I can tell 'im by 'his 'at."

Reference has already been made to the physique of the our men. There have been a few occasions when it has nearly been called into use. One night an Australian nurse was going home, and at the corner she passed three Australians. "Good night, boys," she said. "Goodnight, sister," was the reply. She had not gone far when she was accosted by a civilian who asked if she was alone? The reply, "No. There are three Australians at the corner," was enough to cause the intruder to retreat.

The story of how the Anzacs broke up a peace meeting in the city and held a meeting of their own may not have reached home yet. The promoters of the original meeting were advocating peace at any price when the Anzacs stormed the platform, holding aloft the banner, 'Victory before Peace'. The chairman and supporters fled, and a motion was then put and carried unanimously, deprecating the methods of the "peace party" in seeking peace before the complete submission of Germany. A recruiting meeting in Trafalgar Square was afterwards held.

Too much praise cannot be bestowed on the Australian civilians in England for all they are doing to direct and make enjoyable the stay of convalescent men in England.

The Anzac Club and Buffet catches a man the day he leaves hospital, and if he has no friends, sees that he gets into a good circle, and even a good home for the period of his furlough."

LETTERS FROM THE FRONT

From Sergeant A. Louis Dardel[6]
January 9, 1916

"Back again in good old sunny Egypt and my word, what a treat it is. What a time the boys had when we landed in Alexandria. Though we had Arabs galore over at Anzac, the lads never molested them, even the Greeks were more or less taboo, but the old dinkum Saida (Arab)* as soon as we lobbed in Alexandria! The lads looked on them as so many critters who had enjoyed peace and quiet during all that time we had been away, and it was their bounden duty to forthwith molest them, and so try and make up for the time they had lost, and molest them they did.

I suppose you want to know how we got here. You will know about Anzac anyway, so I needn't say anything about that, but I think Abdul was very glad to be rid of us. We stayed at ---- for three weeks, and then shifted here per S.S. -----.

The natives at ------ seem to exist on cultivation, and their methods are of the most primitive. They use oxen and funny old ploughs, which they take home overnight on the donkey they usually ride."

[6] Aurel (Aurrie) Louis Dardel was one of four brothers who served in World War 1, sons of Helen and James Dardel of Chaumont, Batesford. A few days after receiving notification of a Military Medal being awarded to their son Eric in May 1917, the parents received word that Aurrie had been killed in action in France.

* From Arab word for 'Greetings'

From Private Thomas Desmond Burke[7], Zeitoun Training School, Egypt
January 1, 1916

"Dear aunt,
We have evacuated Gallipoli and for weeks before leaving no mails were sent away. During the last few weeks we suffered badly for want of water and proper food, owing to the rough seas and obstacles in transportation up the gullies during the cold weather. A month before the evacuation all along our front, men were sent away sick, through frost-bite, diphtheria, nervous breakdowns and physically run down for want of proper food. About the end of November there was a cool change, and we did not have dug-outs sufficiently large and comfortable enough to accommodate our men. We got a slight fall of snow, it was not heavy, but effective enough to give us rheumatics, influenza and frostbite, owing to being confined in the trenches and getting very little circulation.

We could not have stayed there much longer. Four of our company were the last to leave. You may say that those who stayed to the last did a glorious action and I would not wish to belittle them in any way, but if volunteers had been called for, I venture to state that 90% of our men would have responded, so to save any jealousy these men were detailed. One of our 18lb artillery guns was blown up at the same time the last party left. I have been told that the mines were not exploded, but it's not for me to criticise.

We went to ----- and stayed two weeks and got our Christmas billies and some mail. We got a pay and bought fruit.

I got an order to pack up and go to Zeitoun for instruction, where four of our battalion are attending. I'll probably be here two weeks more then will have to return to my unit.

---

[7] Thomas Desmond Burke was born in Ireland in 1888. He died in August 1916 after being wounded at Pozieres – just a few months after writing this letter.
Burke had lived in Geelong with his mother, aunt and sister, working at one of the city's chemical plants.

I am in a ragged condition, as I have only the clothes I wore in the trenches and did not receive enough money to buy new ones, though I may get some shortly.

Remember me to all the girls, and if you want to have this published, it is an account of our departure from Gallipoli, and may be of interest to Geelong people, as a number of Geelong men are in our brigade.

T. Burke"

From Staff-Sergeant Gollan, Australian Base Camp, Monte Video House, Weymouth, Dorset
January 19, 1916

"Just a line before I leave England for Egypt. I have now fully recovered from my five months on the peninsula, and am glad to be at work once more. Indications point to ---- as our destination and the members of the draft, which sails in a few days, will rejoin their original units there. The number of Australians in England is decreasing every day, and there are few to be seen about the streets of London now. There is no doubt that the people will miss the distinctive hat and light khaki uniform; the business people and places of amusement will miss our men also, for without a doubt the convalescent Anzac went about his pleasure in England in no half-hearted manner.

Every day, several hundred men, whose term of leave has expired, report back to Headquarters in Horseferry Road, Westminster, and from there are despatched to the International Base Camp at Abbeywood, Kent. The camp is situated on the picturesque Borstal Heath in the midst of the Borstal Woods. It is here that the men are classified. "A" Class are fit for return to the front, "B" class are temporarily unfit, "C" class remain in the army for "home duties" and "D" class are permanently unfit – "PU's"– and await despatch home to Australia. The second class has also the biggest proportion, but by means of gradual stages and in physical drill and route marching they filter through into the drafts. The latter find the training rather severe for the first few days, especially after the time of relaxation and ease.

From Abbeywood, the "A" class men are sent to the South of England, where the final touches are put on prior to embarkation. The country lanes are filled with long lines of Australians on the march, and the villages echo with the strains of their singing.

Whereas in Australia they sang 'Australia Will Be There', now they sing 'The Anzacs Have Been There', and they are going again.

A boat full of wounded unfit for further service left for Australia and received a fitting send-off today. The depot band from Weymouth inspired the farewell with appropriate music. Amongst the officers was Lieut Joe Catron who for several months carried out the duties of Adjutant to the Base Camp. Several months' leave has enabled him to see those at home before his date for return. The man returning to Australia will usually find himself loaded with letters, diaries and parcels for relatives of his mates.

HR Gollan"

LETTER FROM THE FRONT BY HR *[Roy]* Gollan
Published May 25, 1916

"Hospitals in Egypt are empty now, many are shutting. Their former occupants have rejoined their ranks or taken a boat to Australia.

New arrivals in the land of the Pharaohs are rather interested; the old hands are fed up because a year ago they had their fill of the desert and also the attractions of Cairo. But just at present the men are "frightfully" fit (as the Australians put it) and have been trained for action in whatever area they may be sent. Rumour has it in the ranks that Kitchener sent the Australians to Egypt to get some discipline into them and any private in the camp will tell you that he is "full" of it...

It is not an easy matter to get to the Front from Egypt. From Cairo you have to travel by train, motor boat, more train and horse and camel. A hundred and fifty miles away at Beersheba the Turkish headquarters are no nearer their goal than they were a year ago...

A patrol away out in the desert avoids our Light Horse, a spy caught swimming in the Canal—these are the only evidence of a possible attack. Near the waterway itself may still be seen the trenches with the entanglements of barbed wire which resisted the attack of a year ago. New wire has been added to make the barrier more formidable. And though not actually occupied, the troops are camped near to take up residence there should it become necessary.

The problem of transport is met in every possible way, and to continue the journey to the front line one has choice of railway, motor lorry, horse or camel. Running out also are a pipe, a road and a telegraph line. They fade away and become lost in the sandy spaces ahead. As we board the train we see four men sweating at the railway, packing up the sand under the railway. "I was a Bank Manager in New South Wales," said one man, "Now I am a blessed navvy." Yes, they are fed up with the desert— nothing but sand for miles and miles, and then — more sand.

As far as the road runs there is much traffic. The train with narrow waggons and a funny little George Stephenson engine rumbles along. The motor lorries and mule carts come and go, and out on the right there is another little railway and a still narrower gauge. The little trucks are drawn by mules. They carry stone for the road — a friable limestone that binds fairly well after it is watered. Each truck has an Australian and several "gyppies"* on it, one man generally riding postillion. The black and white work cheerily together; Christian and Mohommedan in the common cause.

Mile after mile the six-inch pipe line winds its way across the desert. Presently we come to the rail head and the end of the road. This is not the only rail head: each one is distinguished by a special name in its respective area. Rail head is a centre of activity. Here water and supplies transfer from the mechanical to the camel train. Australian drivers direct both. The officer of the Camel Corps was only a sheep farmer on the Plains of the Wimmera. He could not feel at home in society, but he has been to Anzac, promoted from the ranks, and has an amazing singleness of purpose in his work. He has a wife and three children, and they are beginning to ask already when daddy is coming home. The youngest does not know him.

Somewhere out in the desert, as will be readily surmised, there is a line of defence. As we reach the furthest outpost, we see perched on camels men with rifles and shovels returning from their work. Trenches are in strange contrast to those at Gallipoli. Here the drifting sand was, and always will be, a problem, but it can be dealt with, though it is heart-breaking to find on the morrow that your digging of yesterday has to be done over again, owing probably to a "Khamp Seen" (wind storm) having arisen during the night. Coming back to the rail head we pass the camel trains returning with their empty water cans. In this way in the near east the water problem seems to be ever with us.

Strange though it may seem, the troops on the front line are quite contented.

* Egyptians

Recently a Staff Officer was visiting the men at work. "Well men," he said. "You are to be relieved tomorrow and can come back to camp and have a rest." Noticing no expressions of pleasure he inquired into the reason and was informed that the men had quite settled where they were—they were away from the formality of a standing camp, and nearer the real thing. The new Australian front is there. Whether a shot will ever be fired from it, none of us can say. But we live in hope."

Extracts of letter from Pte AN Royce*
At Sea, April 1st, 1916 [published June 22, 1916]

[*Before going on board at Alexandria*] "...breakfast consisted of bully beef and bread and water, but we enjoyed it all right. We drew into the boat about 7 a.m. and started to unload about 9.30. All the stuff had to be carried some distance the way the boat was lying. I am glad to say we did not have to carry the stuff....

The rest of the unit did not come down until about 10 past 1 and at 4 o'clock, we got relieved. We got a pass and went round to Alexandria and had a look around; we were really too tired to go anywhere."

"[*On board*] ...We have very fine beds on board here; they are swinging, and white sheets. The boat is a hospital ship and is staffed with Tommy orderlies. They are not too bad although we do not see a lot of them. There are a terrible lot of us sick, and it's not so extra rough; I don't know why it is. There was a little leave granted the next day. There was a monitor at anchor just near where we passed. They are not unlike the old Cerberus only they are cut away more at either end. They seem to be only a foot out of water at bow and stern. There was also a battleship and a mine layer in the harbour, also a lot of mine-sweepers. There is a big breakwater round the harbour, and only one entrance. We are very well fed on board. Yesterday we had two life-boat parades; and the sisters have to carry their life-belts with them wherever they go....."

"**Somewhere in France, April 4** — We arrived here this morning, and are now lying at anchor waiting to go into the berth. All our cameras have been taken from us, doctors, sisters, all. We have receipts for them, but when we will get them back, I don't know. I'll miss not having it......"

*Arthur Neil Royce (generally known as Neil), was a young fitter and turner. His father, Geelong YMCA officer Archibald Royce, also enlisted about 18 months later. Both returned safely to Australia.

"Somewhere in France — We arrived here last Wednesday after nearly two days' train journey in "dog boxes", but we are none the worse for it. The first night we spent in a very cold way. Some of the boys in our tent found themselves half outside the next morning. The next day we started to load the train; and that night we got two hours' leave, so we went into town again.

We slept in the goods shed that night, and in the morning finished loading; about half past 12 we left and entrained. There is some bonzer scenery on the way up; some tunnels that took some time to go through. Of course, we were in darkness. The next day, we stopped at a town called Dijon; after dinner we had a route march round town. We were led by a French soldier. He took us to all the interesting parts that were close by. While we were marching through the street, the people were following us; also running from all ways to have a screw at us."

Reportage

Anzac Hostel in the YMCA building in Cairo

SOLDIERS' CLUB
By H R Gollan
June 22, 1916

Two Anzacs camped down on the Canal Zone came to Cairo on special leave. Unfortunately their leave had been granted just before pay day—so each was short, and after a day's sight-seeing they found themselves that night with only a few piastres. Now, to be like this is not a pleasant experience as you soon find out. You start walking round to find a friend to borrow from—and you don't find him. Then you remember that one of your officers is at Shepheard's *[Hotel]*, but you find that he has just been transferred to 'somewhere'. You call on the shop-keeper who has received a few of your piastres—but you learn he is a businessman, not a philanthropist. You are stranded in Cairo.

Thanks, however, to the forethought of Australian friends in Cairo, our two stranded friends found themselves at the Anzac Hostel. You could see they were tired. With fine diffidence they stated that they were stranded, had leave passes but no money and desired advice as to what they were to do to rejoin their unit. The manager started thinking—was this a bona-fide case? Meanwhile, the men's eyes roamed round the spacious concert hall, saw the games of billiards being played, heard the rattle of cups and jingle of glasses from below, noted the bedrooms, saw a soldier come out with a towel over his shoulder en route to the bathroom, and they wondered what place this was they had "blown into".

The manager told them this was the Anzac Hostel, their own Cairo club, started perhaps, without their knowledge, with some of their money. The idea seemed novel. Their own Cairo club? A moment before they were stranded—now in their own club; this great hall, with its lights blazing, a promise of comfort in every corner. The piano going, and, best of all, fellow soldiers to make good company for them.

They were asked to "sign the book" and after inserting their names, numbers and units, were told that some means would be found to get the small amount of cash from their pay later; meanwhile they were able to make full use of the club.

Two very happy soldiers, "sailed" down to the coffee rooms and half an hour later two even happier soldiers lay between the clean sheets of one of the hostel beds. An hour before, they were stranded, now they were part proprietors of this fine club. It is not to be wondered at that they "dreamed of marble halls". Every night there are programs in the concert hall to entertain those in Cairo on leave. How much better is this than that they should roam amongst the subtle attractions of this great city. During interval at a recent concert, given by the Welsh Choir, (a fine combination of singers from the Royal Welsh Fusiliers) the manager of the Hostel told a gentleman who recently visited Cairo—said he: "I have seen the two principal things in Egypt—the Pyramids and the Anzac Hostel. I now go away satisfied." If this incident is not true, it ought to be. It is true as far as the Australian soldiers on leave from the desert are concerned.

– *Geelong Advertiser*

ADVERTISER REPORTER AT THE FRONT SAYS 'WE WANT MEN'

August 8, 1916

"H R Gollan, who went to the Front from the reporting staff of the 'Advertiser', writes—

August 7th, 1916—After the front line went out others knew they were going to their death, yet not a man faltered. Oh I am proud to be an Australian, but will reserve a vivid description of that morning until I see you. There are sad hearts here today, but full of determination to see this thing through.

August 9th—I did not have a wink of sleep for four days, and at the end of that time I was thoroughly exhausted. My work is very nerve trying. I am up about 5.30 and never retire before 11. I do long for just a moment to myself or a nice quiet Sunday. Every day is the same here. It will be terrible when the winter comes. I do wish the whole thing would end. The Germans put up a notice 'Advance Australia if you dare': well, we did dare, and gave them a good taste of what the Australians can do. We want every man to come to our aid."

Driver Cecil Walter Madden in France says there is need of reinforcements—our boys need a spell—go and help them

August 17, 1916

To Mrs MJ Madden— "Harry Groves is in the trenches now. I hope he is a safe. We are all looking to an early end to the war. It is two years on the 19th September since I enlisted. I was with the first of our troops to leave Australia. It seems a long time to you at home waiting, but to me here, moving about from one place to another, makes the time fly.

You would be surprised if you only knew some of the places I have seen and passed through on our way to France. I could keep you going easy for a week telling you the places I have seen, but there is only one place I like best, and that is good old Geelong.

I have not got my furlough yet; suppose I will get it some day.

We want plenty more men here to carry on, so as to give us a spell, but they are not coming, so we have to do the best we can. If you only saw the way the Germans are dug in here, you would not wonder why it takes such a number of men to get them out of France.

I need a change of shirt very badly—have only one shirt. I asked for some more the other day and they issued me with a loose bag! I have not received the parcel of singlets that you said you were sending. Remember me to George Clark, Mr and Mrs McGee and Tom McCoy, also Lieut Catron* whom I met at Mena Camp. He is a very fine chap. Tell Miss ---- her woollen muffler is doing overtime at present, as the weather is very brisk. I have a few souvenirs here, but can't send them along on account of their weight. I tried to send along some English papers, but they sent them back from the military office, and said they had to be paid for."

Roy Gollan writes to his father from France
July 19, 1916

"We are in the midst of shot and shell, and all the incidentals of war. I am quite well, and going strong. A few weeks ago I received a wire to report to the divisional headquarters, and since then have continued doing duty on the staff. For the present

---

*Lt Joe Catron, a keen sportsman, had in 1910 smashed his own world record for endurance skating, a feat achieved at the Geelong Skating Rink.

there seems no prospect of returning to my battalion. My department is looking after and arranging transports within the division and also ammunition. Since I came here I have been working day and night and there is plenty of worry. We have a fine staff. My being detailed here has turned out to be a sort of deliverance, for the very night I came here [Armentieres], ------ went into the trenches and received an awful doing. The Captain, Platoon Sergeant Challis (the famous Carlton footballer), and another officer were killed. We have only two out of six officers in the company. The whole battalion got a warm reception, and in addition, the Germans came across and stole a machine-gun. Our fellows were wild. Harold Graham of Geelong came through without a scratch and smiling. He is as hale and hearty as ever. Personally, I think we are nearing the end of the war. We are strong in men and munitions now. It does one's heart good to hear the continual all-night rumbling of our ammunition waggons. The place is a revelation of organisation. I am sure we shall win. Right is might. Hurrah! Nineteen months' active service, still going strong and always merry and bright."

Carlton football player George Challis was killed at Armentieres the night Roy Gollan arrived, 15 July 1916.

Excerpts from Sgt-Major JSR ['Sam'] Heath, writing to his parents from Egypt [undated; published December 16, 1916]

"Just got your twelve-page letter. Went down to ---- and saw some of our fellows. Had two good swims in the lake—very refreshing in this climate, often 120 degrees in the shade. Still waiting to proceed overseas; it is a bit monotonous but I feel grand.

Have lately come across nine or ten of the old ----- Ambulance chaps, whom I was with on the Peninsula. There is a rumour that our lot will form the nucleus of a new hospital at ------- .

July 31st. Got our order at last and leave here tomorrow, and embark next day in transport for ----. Naturally very joyful, as we've had a bad time here, almost worse than Gallipoli."

From Pte Fred Baverstock, Herne Hill, to his uncle
July 11, 1916

"... The second night in the trenches we had our 'baptism of fire' ... We had to lie flat in the trench and hope against one lobbing in the midst of us. One burst just above us and the two mates on either side of me got hit. One got his hand almost torn off, the other lost three fingers and most of his hand. I was lucky, as the splinters and shrapnel fell all around me and I wasn't even touched. Only knocked out by concussion. Fritz's bombardment lasted an hour and a half and we all got up very shaky; but we gave Fritz a double dose next day. We gave him a huge bombardment on his wires and trenches and then came a 'bonzer' raid, capturing prisoners and frightening hell into them. The next night Fritz gave us a raid, and he was absolutely wiped out. He has left us alone since then for a bit only occasionally giving us a shell or two to let us know he's still there; for every one he gives us we give him six in succession.

We have had some showery weather and there is plenty of mud, but it soon dries up. The nights are short which is good, for it's a strain peering out for a sign of a raid or any other thing that is going on. There are several Geelong boys in my Company and some of them get 'The News of the Week', so I keep acquainted with the doings over in Wattle Land. Our battalion did well in the trenches. One officer got a VC and two privates mentioned for the DCM* but none came my way. So with best wishes to all Geelong boys. Fred."

From Pte William (Bill) Milligan, No 1 Convalescent Camp, Boulogne
August 17, 1916

"Dear Mother and Father, I wrote to you last in the form of a letter before going into the big push. Well, I have been giving Fritz a bit of my weight, and in exchange he gave me a bit of shell. The morning I was going into "stoush", which was in the battle of ----, I saw Roy Talbot, and after him came Gordon Moore. They were both in good health. I was in the party which took rations and supplies to the supports. The battle ground was a dust heap, there was not an inch which had not had a taste of a bomb, it was all disturbed, and the village was not a village, but levelled with the ground. We were shelled a treat. There are other things which I will tell you about when I get back.

* Distinguished Conduct Medal

I with Rob was called on to complete a party to go out in front of the captured positions.* That was "No Man's Land" ... I lost Rob, but kept with four others. ... Rob joined us up a day later, so we were A1.

We were told to get ready to do a bit of business. It was August 4th when the order came round and at 9.15 p.m. we moved out with a "Come on, boys! Hop out and give 'em hell." Well, we came on and we hopped out, but I'm thinking that Fritz gave us the hot climate. I no sooner got over the top when my dial came in contact with a bit of shell which caught me just under my left optic. Vi [sister Violet] always said I had a hard 'dial', and I am convinced she was right, for the bit of iron only knocked a little skin off, so John Willie [referring to himself] kept running forward and succeeded in breaking all running records.

I reached the objective and had started work, when Rob came up. The shell and shrapnel fire were terrible, not to say anything about bombs and machine gun fire. Poor old Rob said as he shook my hand "Goodbye Bill, I'm hit." I told him to go back. He started off and that was the last I saw of him. I was hit shortly after, and made my way safely back to the line, where I was dressed. My wounds are not serious, but shell wounds in the arms and thigh and a few shrapnel wounds on my side near my ribs; the arm being the one I burnt at the cement works.

When in the hospital I saw a cobber, who told me that Rob was carried out on a stretcher. But that was all they could tell me about him. I hope he is not too badly hit. I have been trying to find out where he is, but have failed so far. I don't know where Fred or Les are, and I don't suppose I will receive any home letters, until I get back with the boys.

Kindly let friends know and relatives know how I am situated for the present. I hope you are all in the best of health, and I don't want you to worry too much for John Willie as under my left optic, I am tip top."**

*Private Robert Boyd. He died of wounds at Pozieres August 6, 1916

*Milligan was not as 'tip top' as he told his parents: his eyesight and hearing were both permanently damaged as a result of the head wounds he suffered and he was invalided back to Australia in 1917.

News snippets
August 1916

Letters by last mail from Pte Albert James Saffron* state he is ill in hospital, the result of being buried by a shell. He is being well cared for by a couple of dear Australian nurses and hopes to get back to his unit soon. He congratulates us on getting conscription brought in (he heard it had been passed) and only regrets it was not brought in sooner. He is a strong Laborite, and in the interests of conscription his opinions should influence some of the lads he was acquainted with before he left Australia. He went with the first AIF Battalion and had no rest till invalided. He went to England about March.

Sgt James Thomas Kerley** has sailed for the Front. A compliment was paid him by the officer commanding his company, who appointed him Sergeant-Major on the troopship for the trip. Captain Ernest Spargo, lately senior medical officer at Royal Park camp, and once medical officer at Geelong Camp, has sailed on a troopship for England.

Lt Trevor Williams, formerly engineer at the Geelong Harbour Trust, was in Geelong on Monday on final leave. He is attached to the Pioneer's Battalion now in Sydney and expects to sail in the near future.

Last night he was farewelled at the ABC by some of his engineer friends.

ABC Cafe, Moorabool Street.

Mr Leslie William Taylor, son of Ald George Taylor, Mayor-elect, on Monday enlisted in the AIF and goes into camp at Royal Park in the course of a few days.

*Saffron survived and returned home at war's end.
**Kerley was from the auctioneering firm of Kerleys Auction Rooms in Moorabool Street which operated in Geelong for 110 years, from 1910 until 2020. He also returned home safely, as did Williams and Taylor.

From Private Edwin C Brownhill*
(undated; published October 12, 1916)

"Our sergeant wrote the following article about Ranji Graham [a fellow soldier and amateur boxer]. I think I could not do better than send it. I might say that Ranji has caused me more amusement than anyone else.

'The character I wish to describe is one that stands out from the rest. I always consider him as the CJ Dennis ideal in such pieces as "Doreen", and "Spring Song Of A Bloke". He is dark, small of stature, with a loud voice ('tis said that the Turks know it well) and a gait that is only possible through long contact with what he is pleased to call sports.

George Arthur Graham by name—to us he is Ranji, and worth his weight in gold. A moving spirit amongst the men; popular, and always to the fore with some laughable expression from the vocabulary of the sports. Literally speaking his heart is larger than his head than himself; his spirit is wonderful. On long and trying marches, when big men became slow and silent, and a cheering word and a song was wanted, from whence think you it came? Aye, George Arthur Graham.'

Ranji Graham

From Sgt Robert (Bert) Wilson Gollan

"(Brother of Roy Gollan, who was on the 'Advertiser' staff) writes to his parents in Geelong from Salisbury camp—'Women are taking to a large extent the places of the men, and it is very strange to see girl bus conductors, lift operators, hotel porters, railway cleaners and booking clerks, taxi drivers, munitions workers etc. Men exempt do special police duty, rounding up shirkers etc. At the Anzac Buffet I met Mrs Fisher and Miss Hodinett, both friends of Roy's.

The Anzac Buffet is a place where soldiers can go to read, write, enjoy a little music or gratis get a cup of tea and a sandwich. They are doing magnificent work, helping especially penniless soldiers. Sorry there should be any, but some are fools. We are working hard now on the Salisbury Plain and may soon be going across to France to do our little bit toward the victorious conclusion of the war.'"

*Brownhill's family founded J.C Brownhill and Sons printing firm and had a long association with the 'Advertiser'.

The Anzac Buffet was founded in 1915 by expatriate Australian members of the Australian Natives Association, to provide free food and entertainment to Australian servicemen in London.

From Eric Burgess*
(published October 12, 1916 'Geelong and Western District News')

"Eric Burgess writes to his parents at 124 McKillop Street an interesting letter from France. He ... landed at Gallipoli on 2nd September. In November he was wounded by a bomb and sent to Malta. In March he embarked from Egypt for France, where he has been ever since.

8th August—It is fully 10 days since I last wrote—quite an unusual span to elapse for me without writing, but I can assure you that I have been in such a position that it was not advisable to write until I was out of that position. I have been for 12 days in the hottest part of the whole front line of the great British advance. Therefore, I have delayed writing until now.

I shall not attempt to describe in detail my experiences. Suffice it to say that the Australians gained their objective. The artillery bombardments in some cases reduce men to a state of nervous prostration. I am thankful to say I kept going with the best of them, although at times we were completely exhausted. Part of our work was to carry

*Eric Burgess, 22, and his brother Joe, 25, were both killed in France the following year, on the same day – October 4, 1917.

rations over open country to battalions in the firing line. All the time we were under continual hostile shell fire. Other stretcher-bearers did marvellous work, although their work was far more than they could cope with. I was one of the many volunteers who helped to carry the wounded to their dressing-station. Many of our boys have been recommended (several personal friends of mine) for this particular kind of good work. I do not wish to harrow your feelings or increase your anxiety. To do the reverse has been, and still is, my aim, but I knew you would find out from some other source. However, as I am safe and well, as is also, I believe, dear Joe, and as it will be many weeks before the unit can take the field again, I leave it to you not to worry. Fondest love to mother and yourself."

From Sgt-Major JSR Heath, writing to his parents from Egypt (published October 12, 1916)

"Just got your twelve-page letter. Went down to ----, and saw some of our fellows. Had two good swims in the lakes—very refreshing in this climate of 120 degrees in the shade. Still waiting to proceed overseas, it is a bit monotonous, but I feel grand.

Have lately come across some nine or ten of the old ---- Ambulance chaps, whom I was with on the Peninsula. There is a rumour that our lot will form the nucleus of a new hospital at ----

July 13th: Got our orders at last to leave here tomorrow, and embark next day in transport for -----. Naturally I am pretty joyful, as we've had a bad time here—lots worse than Gallipoli.

Leslie Hodges is away from the battalion at present owing to sickness, but is progressing well in England. France is a beautiful country and it seems an absolute sin to desecrate it with bloodshed. I have been much impressed by the people. They are not the frivolous nation some people think. They all seem fired with patriotism of the highest order. I have hardly seen a single case of that half-hearted fatalism or pessimism which seems to have taken hold of some of our own people.

I find plenty to do whether in the trenches or out of them, as my position of ---- means constant work in regard to the organisation of the battalion. However, it gives me a certain amount of scope for the exercise of what little legal knowledge

I possess, as a large amount of the work re courts martial, etc. falls my way. Roy Gollan is a subaltern in the battalion, and doing very well indeed. He shows a natural aptitude for organising work, and will go far (in fact he has already started on the way to further promotion).

I was awfully sorry to hear of poor Billy Sayer's death[8]. I did not know he was in France until the news of his death reached me. Poor Ralph Barnfather[9], who held a lieutenancy in the battalion, is missing. He was a general favourite and doing very well. Certain well-known footballers will, I am sorry to say, not return home. Sgt George Challis, of Carlton (killed in a raid on our trench by a bomb), Sgt Nolan (Richmond)[10], Corporal Fred "Cherry" Douglas (of Chilwell)[11], little "Plugger" Landy[12], who played for St Mary's and Geelong, "Waxy" Campbell[13], of Chilwell, and others have gone down in action. Norman Grigg is with our transport at present. An old injury made it impossible for him to stay in the line on account of heavy marching, so he is now a driver.

Please forgive this disjointed screed, as I have been interrupted several times while writing, and with the usual accompaniments of trench warfare and various people coming in with requests for everything from a pin to an issue of rum, I really forget what I intended to write about. I will write again soon.

P.S. The 'NOW' is seen literally in hundreds of copies in our battalion.

[8] William (Billy) Thomas Sayer was the son of JW Sayer, founder of the Geelong Gallery. Billy took up mining and metallurgy after leaving Geelong Grammar. He was killed in June 1916, age 27.

[9] Andrew Ernest Ralph Barnfather, a carpenter before the war, was a prominent rower with Barwon Rowing Club. Barnfather was killed at Armentieres on July 19, aged 24.

[10] Bill Nolan was a highly regarded footballer, playing two seasons for Richmond before he enlisted in  July 1915. One year later, on July 23, 1916, he died of wounds sustained at Fleurbaix, France.

11 Corporal Frederick Charles 'Cherry' Douglas, a neighbour of Ralph Barnfather's in Clarendon Street, Chilwell, was killed in action at Pozieres (a week before Barnfather's death), on July 14 1916, aged 24.

12 Talented footballer William Joseph ('Plugger') Landy, a shop assistant in Geelong, got in two games for Geelong as an 18-year-old before enlisting in the war. He had served only five months when he was killed at Fromelles on July 19 1916, aged 19.

13 William ('Waxy') Campbell was a labourer before the war. His mother had died when he was a child and he, his father and brother were cared for by a cousin in Myers Street, Geelong.
William died from wounds on July 17 1916 and was buried at Estaires Communal Cemetery near Armentieres, northern France.

Mr and Mrs FM Douglass received a letter from their son, 2nd Lieut Monte Douglass

October 20 1916 — "I am presently on the casualty list, having tripped over a wire and got several bits of skin knocked off; nothing serious, and will be all right in a couple of days." He also stated that he had met his cousin, 2nd Lieut George Douglass.

Mrs Douglass also received word from her other son, Driver Leslie Douglass, who is well. She also heard from driver Keith Howe, who was wounded some time ago, and has been in hospital in Weymouth, England, and is getting better—is going on 14 days' furlough; he says he is longing to be back with the boys on the Front.

Mr Oswald Field, Latrobe Terrace, Chilwell, has received a cable-gram from his brother Pte Hilton Field, of the 58th Battalion, to say that he has been wounded in the left leg and right foot, and is in hospital in London. This is the third time that he has been wounded. *[Returned home a few months later]*

Mrs *[Ellen]* Ellis of Mount Duneed has received a cable from her son, Pte Allan Ellis, to the effect that he is suffering from a slight gunshot wound in the scalp, and is in the Southern General Hospital, London. *[Returned home 1919]*

Mrs WE *[Catherine]* Palmer, Newtown, has received notice that her son, Cpl Frank Palmer, has been wounded a second time. *[Returned home 1918 still carrying injuries to leg]*

Lance-Cpl Ben Esposito
[Undated; published October 12, 1916]

"L-Cpl Esposito is the nephew of Mrs Chisholm of the Coffee Palace, Ocean Grove. He wrote on the eve of the Big Push on the Somme—

"The time has come when we either put 'paid' to Fritz's account or else he pays us. Our lads have been into it already, and have taken some of his trenches; they got cut up, but did good work. Our time comes in a few days and we hope to keep up the good name of Australia. If anything happens to me, do not worry, but think of the rest of the dear kids and perhaps I'll see dear "Mooty" *[brother Mervyn]* again. He died doing his duty, and his brothers will do theirs...."

The following letter was evidently written after the fighting, and in it Esposito states he has come out all right.

"As you know, we have been giving Fritz a pretty hot time. Our lot held a raid the other night, which I was in. From start to finish it was one ear-splitting crash. We must have greatly annoyed Fritz, as we put into him about 5000 shells. Fritz went mad, and sent us over all sorts and sizes of shells. Being one of the audience, I failed to see the joke, and the rest of our chaps got annoyed also; so we gave him something to think about. It was better than football, that rush across "No Man's Land". We killed about 100 of the Germans, and took six prisoners, and all sorts of booty, such as papers, helmets, rifles, etc, and then we came back.

When I say came back, you can bet I was stepping some. It was about 400 yards to go through shell holes, barbed wire and pools of water, and with Fritz speeding us a fond farewell. I'll bet he was pleased when we left.

Everybody behaved tip top. They were a great lot of lads. Take away Fritz's artillery and we could eat him. The officers concerned did their job well. I was very lucky, a machine gun outed a sergeant next to me; it must have jammed then, or our artillery knocked the Germans out.

I think lots of those chaps who are playing football in good old Australia now could come and lend a hand, although we haven't much time for those enlisting now. They get a lot of praise in the papers, but the hard work seems over, so we call them long-thinkers. Tell everybody to cheer up, as every cloud has a silver lining."

From Sgt Bert Gollan

"These verses admirably describe our situation here, and we have now been here a month. The training is hard, but I am still going strong, like Johnny Walker whisky. Have met several of our cousins in England, and Reginald Gollan of Woolwich will probably write to Ernie. Am having a good time and quite well."

"LARK HILL CAMP

There's an isolated, desolate spot I'd like to mention,
Where all you hear, is "Stand at Ease",
"Slope Arms", Quick March," "Attention."
It's miles away from anywhere, by Gad, it is a rum 'un.
A chap lived there for fifty years and never saw a woman.

There are lots of little huts, all dotted here and there,
For those who have to live inside, I've offered many a prayer.
Inside the huts, there's RATS as big as any nanny goat,
Last night a soldier saw one trying on his overcoat.
It's sludge up to the eyebrows, you get it in your ears,
But into it you've got to go, without a sign of fear,
And when you've had a bath of sludge, you just set to and groom,
And get cleaned up for next Parade, or else, it's
"Orderly room!"

Week in week out, from morn till night, with full pack and a rifle,
Like Jack and Jill, you climb the hills, of course that's just a trifle.
"Slope Arms," "Fix Bayonets," then "Present,"
They fairly put you through it.
And as you stagger to your hut, the Sergeant yells, "Jump to it."

With tunics, boots and putties off, you quickly get the habit,
You gallop up and down the hills just like a bloomin' rabbit.
"Heads backward bend," "Arms upward stretch," "Heels raise,
Then "ranks change places,"
And later on they make you put your kneecaps where you face is.

> *Now when this War is over and we've captured Kaiser Billy,*
> *To shoot him would be merciful, and absolutely silly,*
> *Just send him down to Lark Hill, there among the rats and clay,*
> *And I'll bet he won't be long before he drops and fades away.*
> *But we're not down-hearted yet, No."* —from a World War 1 postcard

Bert Gollan, writing from Salisbury, England, to his parents
November 1916

"...*[regarding conscription]* —Last week I recorded my first vote—for the Government having power to call up men of the Commonwealth as they saw the need in the present crisis. I was opposed to conscription, but now I think the volunteers -------- military system has practically been blown out, and other means must be adopted to bring forward forces to permanently crush the Hun. I am a cold-footer* (wore two pairs of socks all last week and then couldn't keep warm!) but men are needed, and will be needed until peace and victory are eventually ours.

My letters are coming through regularly and so far received every one; I will soon need a private secretary — 20 last mail and 11 this, over 50 having arrived in England, and I have written 150 since leaving Australia! We are kept busy, and my letter-writing is done after lights out or on Sundays, after Church parade and inspection.

Our work for the week was five days in the trenches. A farm house was the rendezvous of a few of the sergeants, and for a few shillings, enjoyed quite a little home life, and fared better than stew and bread and jam. Wednesday there was an attack, and our company formed supports, we were lying in the field from about 2 a.m. until 4 or 5, and quite enjoyed it (I don't think), came home and took off my boots for the first time in a week. On Wednesday our mail came in, and I was detailed to instruct a squad in bayonet fighting. On Thursday we took over the trenches, and my job was with a digging party from midnight till 4 a.m. The boys did dig, otherwise they would have been frozen. We are hoping to get four days' leave very soon.

I am trying to work out the Scotland trip. I had a letter from Roy last week. He is still in France and attached to the headquarters. He has a second star and hopes soon to be an adjutant. He certainly has made good since Gallipoli.

*Word-play relating to a term for those who did not want to fight, 'cold-footers'.

My girl friends keep me well posted up with printed matter and newspapers.

The night is cold and I am turning in early for a good sleep. This will practically be our Christmas mail, and I take this opportunity of wishing you a very merry Christmas, and may 1917 have joy and success the whole way through. Am well, very well, and send love to all at home. The war news is most encouraging, and I think the end is in sight, although, perhaps, twelve months off.   Bert."

News Snippets

Mrs Anne Martin received a letter from the Methodist chaplain referring to the death of her son, Gunner Edwin McAllister Martin, in France
"A large company of his former comrades gathered at the burial service, and there was not a dry eye in the bronzed weather-beaten group. Gunner Martin was well respected and liked by all who came into contact with him. He has given his life in a noble cause, and will not go unrewarded."

"Mrs [Winifred] Sullivan of Verner Street, East Geelong, received a cable from her son, Sgt James Sullivan, of the 24th Battalion, stating that he was well, and had been given a commission. Lieut Sullivan left Australia on 8th May 1915, and was at the evacuation of Gallipoli. It speaks well for his stamina that after 18 months' active service he is still fit for duty.*

"At the recent football match between Australia and England, which was played at the Crystal Palace Grounds *[London]* before the King and a large gathering of prominent military officials, several Melbourne players took part. Lieut Sloss, of South Melbourne, was captain of the Australian team, and Lt Billy Orchard (Geelong) had the satisfaction of kicking the winning goal, and also played the best game on the ground."

Billy Orchard played for Geelong in the VFL between 1906 and 1915 and captained the team for two years. He was also playing coach in 1914.

*James Sullivan, a law clerk, was later killed in action at Montbrehain in France on October 5, 1918, just five weeks before the end of the war. He had by this time achieved the rank of Captain.

"Mrs G *[Jane]* Spendlove of 46 Saffron Street, Chilwell, has been advised by the Defence Department that her son, Pte W H (Will) Spendlove, has been seriously wounded (gunshot) in the back, and is now in the Southern General Hospital Westminster, London.*

"Word has been received that Pte Thomas Chester Read who enlisted from Moolap has been seriously wounded in the left arm and right thigh on November 29th."**

Mrs William Petrass of Ormond Road, East Geelong, received a letter this week from Mrs Ruth Harris, Hyde Park, London

"…a line to tell you that your son Corpl William Henry *[Bill]* came to see me twice whilst on leave in London. I was so delighted to see him. He is looking so well, and assured me that he thoroughly enjoyed his leave.

I was so pleased to congratulate him on the honour he has won in receiving the Military Medal. How proud you must be of him. My husband, who is the commanding officer of the company, speaks highly of him and says he is marked for promotion. He always looks so happy and smiling, but, like us all, will be only too pleased when the war is over and we are headed for Australia."

*Spendlove's injury was severe and he was not returned to frontline duty; he returned home in early 1919.
**Read recovered and returned home safely at the end of the war.

ROBERT (BERT) WILSON GOLLAN

Robert Wilson Gollan

Drummer boy Bert, Bendigo, 1910

Bert Gollan, 1916

Bert in army portrait, 1916.

'NEWS OF THE WEEK' 1917

"Lieut RW Gollan of the citizens' forces, Melbourne, son of Mr R Gollan of Elizabeth Street, Geelong West, has enlisted as a ranker in the AIF. His brother, Sergt Roy Gollan, enlisted from the 'Advertiser' Staff."

— *News of the Week October 16, 1917*

AUSTRALIANS IN LONDON HAVE A GOOD TIME

Sergt Bert Gollan wrote to his parents under date November 15 1916; the letter was published February 4, 1917, as follows:

"...had four days leave and such fast days they were too! Took advantage of the opportunity of a trip to Scotland to see the Inverness folk. It was mighty hard going, and I travelled about 1300 miles for twenty-four hours up there. However, it was well worthwhile, and I would not have missed it for something.

I left camp at 8 a.m. on Friday morning. Left Euston station at 2 p.m. and travelling all night, reached Inverness at 6 a.m. next morning. I was aboard the Flying Scotsman, and what a train, too! Sixty miles an hour—some going! Cannot see the names on the stations as the train whizzes past, and the telegraph poles are like fence posts.

When I arrived I went to the Royal Hotel, and taking possession of the bathroom, had the most exquisite shave and wash. Imagine, after five months away from civilization on the Plain and getting back to a 3ft square mirror and marble wash stand. To 'top up' I lined into the breakfast—the Inverness' best—with a captain and several naval officers, and one Australian.

Had beautiful porridge—Scotch "meal" not flaked stuff—and finished up with bacon and eggs. Just fancy the delightful change; soldiers appreciate it after bread and jam and stew. By 9 o'clock I was ready and presentable to make myself known to my Scotch cousins and made my way to meet Belle at the Post Office.

Next went to Harrowden Road and met her mother, such a dear old lady. It is beautiful to hear her talk about "the poor laddie from Australia" and the "bright moonlight nicht, ye ken."

Her daughter is nice, too; she took me around and showed me the places of interest in the city. Scotland is so beautiful with its rugged scenery and innumerable streams and waterfalls.

Met other friends. They were very nice; had tea and spent Saturday evening with them. There are bonny girls in Scotland, and especially Inverness; but Australia is still the first place. I left for homeward journey at 11 a.m. Sunday morning and came home via Glasgow and Edinburgh. It was a wonderful trip and I shall always remember that weekend as one of the pleasantest in my short experience. Arrived in London 7 a.m. on Monday morning. I saw and said goodbye to London friends.

The Lord Mayor's Show was on last week in London and one of the features of the procession was a squad of "Anzac" Light Horsemen. The "Anzacs" have easily first place here in England. The Australians are some class.

Next week we go to ---------, where all the others are, and then the time for action will come. I am well and very happy in the thought and confidence of a safe and speedy return to Australia.

Other snippets from the same issue of the newspaper—

[Regarding the death of Thomas Burke] "….His heart was always in his work, and in April when he was wounded, he would not go to hospital for a couple of days until his wound became septic, and I made him go. I do not know the exact circumstances of his death as I myself was wounded on August 6th, and have only just left hospital. If I can find out I will let you know. He was promoted to corporal on the field three days before he was hit, for good work in action. May the knowledge that he gave his life for the Great Cause, for which we are all prepared to make the same sacrifice, be some comfort to you in this hour of grief. He died a worthy son of Australia.

Yours truly, Victor C. Alderson—Lieutenant."

From soldier Richard Beath to his mother in Chilwell
"—In a little dugout in France, January 29, 1917
"You will be pleased to hear that I have received further promotion.* I have been promoted to the rank of sergeant. I have not yet met Larry or Arthur although I have been trying to find them. You would laugh to see the Huns surrendering. They will put up a fight if they are six to one, but if it is even sides they won't fight at all, but throw down their rifles and put up their hands and beg for mercy. We can beat their infantry with a stick."

From their son, William, who is at Wandsworth, London
"—Mr Fleet of Lonsdale St, Geelong, received the following letter which proves our soldiers are royally entertained in England.
"....I see that Arthur** *[brother]* was buried in Bailleul, that's in Belgium just behind where I was in the trenches. If you look on the map you will see it's pretty near in line with Lille and Dunkirk....

I am having a grand time over here now. Went to the Princess Theatre last week and saw Seymour Hicks and Elaine Terriss in 'Broadway Jones' and it was lovely. The directors of the Bank of Australia had their windows fixed up in such a way that about 30 of us could see the procession. Then after the Show was over they took us upstairs and gave us dinner. Talk about a Banquet; it was grand! I will send you a menu as a souvenir. Twenty-five of us went for a ride around London in a char-a-banc finishing up at the London Opera House to see who was there. We had tea there and got home about 8 o'clock. I will send you the photo of us when I get one, which I think will not be difficult.

Going for another trip on Saturday if all goes well and, mind you, it's all invitations at the expense of the people of the big city. Don't suppose I will be here much longer now, as I am feeling pretty fit and getting fat, which is a good job, as I needed it. Had a letter from Don; he says he is well, but sorry he cannot get along to see me as he is too far away. I received seven letters today; the first for a long time and I tell you they are better than all your medicines for bucking one up."

*Richard Holly Beath had three serving brothers. References are to brothers Lawrence and Arthur.
**Arthur Gunn Fleet – a fireman prior to the war. He died of wounds 23 July 1916. His brothers Donald (Navy) and William returned home safely.

Mr and Mrs Stokes of Chilwell learn that their son, Pte Robert Stokes, has been invalided for the second time suffering from trench feet. He was admitted to the War Hospital at Guildford on December 4th.

Private EJ Camp has been wounded the second time in France and is now in the 5th Southern General Hospital suffering from trench feet and severe gunshot wounds in right arm and leg.*

Mrs Keene, late of Geelong, has received a cable from France that her husband (Ben) is in the trenches doing well. His little daughter, Ethel, has just recovered from a bad attack of meningitis.

Private Henry Penglase is well after being in the trenches for seven months. He is expecting leave soon to visit Mrs Keene's people in London. Mrs Keene has also received word that her youngest brother, Private Albert Morris, has been seriously wounded and his leg broken. Her other brother, Private Joseph Morris, is still in hospital with a weak heart.

From Sgt Bert Gollan to his brother *[Ern]* in Geelong West
February 1 1917
"Now I am writing after a spell of about twelve days in dugouts in France. For four days we did all fatigues for the rest of the battalion. It was a great game carrying rations and fuel to the front line. We were going all night and half the next morning. Last night we came out for a short spell and today I had a bath. A week in the trenches and a fellow feels like a creature from the jungle. For three days I was on an isolated post seventy yards from Fritz's trench and did not relish the job too much. Had he come over he would have been greeted with a few grenades.

One day we got a good doing from his artillery with "whizz bangs" and high explosives. Not much damage was done; one casualty, and several rapid changes in the position of our dugouts. My overcoat and equipment were hanging on a peg in

---

* Ernest John Camp recovered and returned to Geelong.

the trench when a "Minnie" came gracefully over. You can see the shell coming; this one was a "dud", lucky for a few in the vicinity, and came straight for the "possey". My narrowest squeak was missing machine gun fire by a few inches. I was taking a party with ammunition to the front line and had to pass a gap in the trench. Fritz had a machine gun trained on the spot. I nearly had to stand for the remainder of my life, but I got down very quickly and the lead disfigured the side of the trench instead.

That is only what is occurring to us every day when in the parapet. "Joe" is the name given to the German machine gun and he is some class; plays 'Home Sweet Home' on his gun, but our boys find him and play to him "the dead march from Saul". You have no idea to what extent France has been devastated, and for many, many years she will bear the marks of this mighty upheaval, tons of barbed wire and shell holes innumerable.

Sox are a problem in mud and water knee and thigh deep, it is impossible to keep dry feet. We have high gum boots (rubber) which do a great deal towards keeping our feet dry. Have heard nothing of *[brother]* Roy yet, but hope to see him soon."

Another soldier also writes— "...socks are what we need. There is no chance of drying them and our feet are always wet. Tell our friends to send them in any quantity. They will be more than welcome. I am writing in an enemy's dugout, 30 ft. down, and feel very much like a rabbit. It is fitted with bunks similar to those on board ship. The ground all round is riddled with shell holes. The mud—well it sticks closer than a poor relation! I have met several Geelong boys including Burns, Bechervais, Volum. All glad to see each other 'fit' and well. A lance-corporal from our company was hit in the ear and nose and had to go to hospital. I was offered a commission in Egypt, but we were just leaving for France so I did not get it. I also met Lieut Wilfred Jackson; his father was an inspector of schools in Geelong some time ago. Write soon again. I far prefer letters to meat."

February 8: Mr Gollan has received a cable that his son Lieut and Adjutant Roy Gollan is reported wounded in France.

February 8: Sgt Robert Gollan has received a commission.

February 22: mention of Roy Gollan's wounding, 54th Battalion — slight gunshot wound.

March 1: Adjutant Roy Gollan, who was admitted to the 14th Military Hospital in Horseferry Road, London, on January 7th suffering from wounds to the chest caused by a high explosive shell, has been operated on and his father on Thursday received a cable: "Operation successful. Doing well."

March 29: Mr. Gollan of Geelong West has received word that 2nd Lieut Robert Gollan, who was reported seriously ill, is now well at Boulogne and that his brother, Adj. Roy Gollan, slightly wounded, is in hospital in England.

SNIPPETS, 'NEWS OF THE WEEK'

From Roy Gollan to his parents
March 29, 1917

Mr and Mrs Gollan have received word from their son. The letter was written on his behalf by Chaplain A R Home. He says—"You will like to have a line as soon as possible to show how I was wounded. A shell burst quite close to me in the trench, and the fragment hit my side, about two inches above my right breast. This was on January 24th. I came straight down here and am comfortably tucked into bed with plenty of attention. They tried to find the bit of metal in me on the 25th, and am glad to say we were successful, and I am now on the high way to recovery. The bit passed through my pocket-book and this no doubt saved me from more serious injury. As it is, I lie quietly, being in no pain except when they dress the wound.

I am only waiting for the ambulance train to take me down to the base and then to Blighty, I cannot write myself just yet, as it makes my right arm stiff. That is only a matter of a week or two.

Don't worry. I am not in the least bad and am not sorry to be in a warm place. I have got the piece safely to show you when I come home, to keep as a souvenir."

Mr James McCann of Hope Street has received cheery letters from his two sons, Dave and Percy. Pte Dave McCann is again at the Front, after having been in hospital for a brief period suffering slightly from shell shock. He was so fortunate to be treated by Dr McPhee*. He is very confident that the war will finish this year as Fritz is now 'on the run'. Papers come very irregularly, but the more fortunate Geelong boys all back one another up with their copies. Percy, of the 29th Battalion, writes very cheerily from Salisbury Plain and reports that Sgt Kerley is well and very popular amongst the men. He also sends regards to Geelong friends.

Pte Leo Carter writes that he came out of the trenches all right a couple of days ago; later, while doing fatigue duties, a shell burst close by and a fragment struck him on the right cheek.

Private Percy Rowley is returning to Australia very shortly. He has been away two years, was at the evacuation of Gallipoli, and was in France until sent to England with pleurisy. He has been three months in hospital.

Lieut Roy Gollan — presented to the King at Buckingham Palace
April 19, 1917

"This letter has been received from Lt Adjutant Roy Gollan, of the 'Advertiser' staff, by his parents—

February 18: Dear Father, You will be delighted to hear that I have so far recovered as to be presented to the King and Queen yesterday afternoon, when I spent a most enjoyable time. There were 25 of each — the Australians, New Zealanders and Canadians, all wounded officers in the convalescent stages. We went to the Palace in motor ambulances, and were met in the main reception hall. From there we went to the palace ballroom (where all the ladies are presented at court.)

Here a noted professor, who had just returned from an expedition to discover the source of the Amazon river, gave a most intellectual and instructive lecture, telling of his experiences.... Ladies and duchesses moved about amongst us, and were most free

---

*Dr Robert George McPhee, who practised in Ryrie Street, Geelong, for over 40 years. McPhee enlisted in 1916 at the age of 39.

and informal. The lecture was illustrated with moving pictures. At the conclusion we were each presented to and shook hands with the King and Queen, also the Duchess of Connaught.

Afternoon tea followed in the supper room after which we adjourned to the lounge where the King and Queen moved about and chatted amongst the assembled officers. I had a chat for about ten minutes with the Queen. She asked all about my experiences in Egypt and France and was very interested to know that I had come from the ranks. I did not actually speak to the King but was in his presence the whole time and heard him talking to others. The Duke of Connaught was much interested in my pocket-book, through which the fragment passed into my chest. The gathering dispersed at 6.30 p.m. The Palace is a most magnificent place and the whole proceedings bucked us all up wonderfully, especially when thanked personally by their Majesties for what we had done and suffered. I am well on the mend now and will be returning to the battalion in a few weeks. My London friends have been to see me and I am keeping in touch with the paper people in Fleet Street."

Mr David Rhind of 'Chevy', Wallington, received a cable from his son, Lance-Cpl Hector Rhind, intimating that he is now Gas Bombing Instructor. He says his son: "finished the gas course on Wednesday with a written exam—two hours in the morning and afternoon on the gas. There were three Australians and six English NCOs and I'm pleased to say that when the results were published, the three Australians held the first three places with Lance-Cpl Rhind on top. He scored the possible number of marks — 100."

Driver J Adams of the Australian Artillery, writes — "This happened in France. A party of us had got up to the firing line with a mob of fresh horses. The noise of the guns upset them badly, and a number of them stampeded. In the confusion, I was thrown down a bank of a ditch, and the horses that a man named Laidlaw* was holding backed down nearly on top of me. I ... could not get out without being trampled on by these horses, so if Laidlaw had let them go I was done for, but he held on to their heads for nearly an hour. Though the strain on his arm would have been bad till help came, and the horses and myself were got up safely. Had Laidlaw let the horses go, I must have

---

* Believed to refer to Robert Laidlaw, station manager of 'Newlands', Apsley, before the war.

been trampled to death. He kept saying we would be all right and would 'hang on'; for days after he was so stiff we had to help dress him. I am writing this to let his friends know how he saved my life, as from the little I have seen of him I don't think he would tell you about it himself.

After we parted I picked up your paper which I saw him reading. I hope you get this and his friends know how he acted, as it is the only way I can show my thankfulness. Now we have parted and I might never see him again. He is a real white man, and always ready to give a hand to someone who did not know too much. I think some of us were nearly as frightened as the horses."

LETTER TO THE EDITOR
A wounded soldier's plea

"Sir, I am writing with great pleasure a few lines to you. I have my heart and soul in the cause, although I have been permanently injured. There is no doubt this is a just and righteous cause. All honour is due to those who have given up all to fight the good fight for freedom and justice, to uphold the flag and their country's honour and to defend their loved ones at home in the hour of danger. How some take up the "conscientious view" I do not know, but I feel sure it is far better for a man to sacrifice his own life than lose the remainder of his family at home.

We must honour our boys to the full, for the best this earth can give would not repay them for their services rendered to defend their loved ones at home, and the country all the boys on the S------ are so proud to belong to. And I must not forget the lads that have died a noble death for us all. But in death they live, for if they are not with us on the earth, they still seem to us all to have that smile — if not the earthly smile, it's that bright and happy face with a smile which is the old smile, from above.

Keep smiling, for we are going to fight the true good fight until we win that victory, above all victories, which will come in its own time to our own land, from this land across the sea, and we shall all enjoy that bright sunshine in peace. And I say from my heart, knowing how hard it is, we must all do our bit. – S/smith DC Ellis*.

*Shoeing smith David Charles Ellis, of Geelong West

—*Geelong Advertiser* April 17, 1917

**2nd Lieut Bert Gollan writes to his parents
April 24, 1917**

"You ask why the soldier's vote "No" *[to conscription]* was so large. The answer is that the vote was taken while we were in England. No officers were allowed to speak to the men on the subject; plenty of them knew absolutely nothing, and it was their first vote. They said, 'What fools we were to join the Army.' They are out of it, good luck to them. Why should I vote Yes and make them come? I said to them that numbers would hasten the end, and why should they endure the hardships longer than otherwise? They had a taste of the Army, why not give the slackers at home a taste too? A good many voted the same as their pals, giving the matter absolutely no thought. A vote taken now would be very different. They have seen devastated and ruined France, been in the trenches, shelled and sniped at by the enemy, lost pals, suffered mud, and had unwholesome food, fearful cold days without sleep.

There were not sufficient men for reliefs, double shifts etc. They have seen the real thing and wish for the end. I have been doing my bit and a little over because of some of the slackers still in Australia.

Yesterday I saw quite a lot of Boche prisoners, just in from our last success at Grandcourt. They were awfully young, about 18 or 20; one we asked was 21 and had not started to shave yet; one Boche Sergeant, when asked about the War, said he did not think they were still winning, but what he wanted to know was how badly they were going to lose. I also saw Boche officers. They don't seem at all elated at their chance of winning the war. One said he heard of food shortages in Germany, but

Campaign poster encouraging new recruits, 1915.

In mid-1916, enlistment levels had fallen to the lowest level yet. High casualty rates, a longer-than-expected conflict, and a fall in enthusiasm for the war combined to create a potential policy problem for the government in sustaining the war effort. A plebiscite on conscription was held on 28 October 1916. It sparked a divisive debate that split the public and resulted in a close but clear rejection of the measure.

Artist Norman Lindsay produced several posters for the pro-conscription campaign, including this one.

the troops in the trenches had plenty to eat. German organisations made provision for that. I have seen some of the latest things to be used in driving the Boche back, and they are 'wonderful' and 'awful'. I am proud to be a Britisher."

A snippet
Private Roy writes to the Editor from a troopship at sea and asks the Editor that his message be given to the school children of Geelong—and especially of Swanston Street, which he attended four years ago—"We are just going to do our little duty to defend mothers, wives, sisters and school children as well as to fight for King, Country and Australia."

'Lieut Gollan again in the Firing Line'
Lieut-Adjutant Roy Gollan writes to his parents
March 24, 1917
"Am feeling very fit and gone back to my battalion. My division was the first into Bapaume. Shall I ever forget the Somme? I feel very sore about your Parliament men squabbling about amongst themselves when such big issues are at stake in the world conflict. The fact that Australia is not represented at the great Empire War Conference at present being held in London, and all because of internal strife in Australia, makes all Australians over here feel ashamed in the eyes of the world."

Lieut Gollan met his brother, 2nd Lieut Robert Gollan, after two and a half years. Robert writes:
"At last I have seen the long lost brother, after chasing him round for several months. I followed him to hospital to find he had gone to England, and now in the base camp we have met and enjoyed each other's company for several days. He goes back to the line tomorrow (April 2nd), he is looking very well and is as lively as ever, and still possesses that continuous whistle of his. I went to camp and simply followed the whistle. He is, if anything, thinner; I forgot I had grown and am now as tall as he.

We were in the afternoon together, and had our photos taken. He has knocked about and seen everything to be seen, and met many nice people and broadened his mind and ideas immensely. He certainly had a narrow escape.

"Roy met a sergeant, a Geelong boy. He was one of a firm of auctioneers *[Kerley]*, and was on the recruiting committee prior to coming here. I have also seen Harold Riddell. Funny how I came across him; in censoring some letters I saw Harold's name mentioned, and on following it up found the man I wanted, and made myself known to him. He is a fine fellow. He won the DCM by throwing a fusing shell out of a pile of 300 others and thus saving a large supply of ammunition and many lives. He has had many narrow escapes; has been buried; a bullet grazed his chest, taking away his tunic pocket and leaving him untouched. They are forming a 6th Australian Division now in England. *[Harold and Mervyn Riddell were Gollan cousins]*

I shall be glad to receive the 'News of the Week'. Am quite well and back next week to firing line."

"Notes on the late Sgt Blanksby—A note relating to the death of her husband. Mrs Beatrice Blanksby *[of Fitzroy Street, Geelong]* received the following from Warrant Officer J. McGain —

"I have no doubt you have heard long before this that Les has met with a terrible accident …. In Les I had one of the best friends a man could wish for, and words cannot tell how I miss him. He was so amiable and unselfish, and would take on even duties that were not due to his rank. His one object was to serve the King and his Country as well as he could, and I can say without fear of contradiction that he did it well. If ever I was pushed for a good NCO to take charge of any men or guard, I knew that poor old Les would be willing to do it and do it well, even if it was not his turn. The circumstances of the case are very painful to me, but I think you ought to know the result of the court inquiry into the accident -----"*

> *Leslie Holmes Blanksby, an engineer, was with a group of soldiers returning to camp after a night out in Belgium. Their vehicle rolled into a ditch. Blanksby and another soldier stayed with the vehicle while the rest of the men set off to walk back to camp. When they returned to pick up the pair the next morning, they were horrified to find them deceased. The men had died of exposure during the cold March night.
>
> Blanksby's younger brother Harold had been killed a month earlier in France.
> Their father was one of the founders of the original Labour Party in New South Wales and a former member of the NSW parliament.

Roy and Bert Gollan in March 1917, when they were able to spend a few days together after not seeing each other for 2½ years.

'AUSTRALIANS'

We are not cotton spinners all,
but some love England and her honour yet.

We stand on the shore of Durban
And watch the transports go
To England from Australia,
Hurrying to and fro,
Bearing the name of a nation
Who are heroes to the core,
To stand and fall by the Motherland
And they are sending thousands more.

We've watched the ships returning
With the cripple and the main,
With limbs that rail and falter,
Theirs is an immortal name.
The deathless name of 'Anzac'
That thrills from pole to pole.
The remnants of the heroes
On the long and glorious roll.

And now in their tens of hundreds
Come the man to fill their ranks,
And what can we do to show them
Our love, our pride and thanks?
We can't do much (I own it)
But give them a passing cheer —
While the real elite beat a shocked retreat,
Why, they saw one drinking beer!

The path the Anzacs went,
Could they rest in their beds at night time?
Or live in their damned content?
Could they talk with a sneer of Australians
Where one or two get drunk,
I rather a drunk Australian
Than a wealthy Durban funk!

He is a better man than you are
You dear teetotal saint.
You do not drink, you will not fight
What wonderful restraint.
We stand on the shore of Durban
For we're not all made like you
And the glorious name of 'Anzac'
Thrills us through and through.

By EMC 1916

Written by Ethel M. Campbell in South Africa upon hearing a wealthy Durban merchant speak disparagingly of Australians.
Campbell (1866-1954) was known for her enthusiastic greetings and farewells of Australian troop ships in Durban during World War I. She later became well known as a poet and author in South Africa.
She visited Australia to great acclaim from former soldiers in 1923.

July 5, 1917: Bert Wounded Mr Gollan has been notified by the Defence Dept that his second son, Lieut R W (Bert) Gollan has been wounded; nature not stated. He was previously in hospital with a sprained ankle and had just returned to his battalion.

Casualty Lists No. 318, 319 contain 2053 names including — Wounded: Lieut Robt W. Gollan.

August 8: Brother met in France after 2½ years' service. Both have been wounded in France.

Lieut Robert Gollan wrote from Paris to his parents
August 15, 1917

"I am in Paris on ten days' leave. Little did I imagine that I would see so much, but the awful experiences that I have been through have been well repaid and forgotten, in the thoughts of so much that is worthwhile that has happened to me since leaving bonnie Australia. I did not appreciate Australia until I left it. Now I know it to be the nicest, cleanest place and the sooner we can return the quicker and better, for it is the only place in the world for me.

We left the line in the early morning. I was as excited as a schoolboy on holidays, and the night before I thought that every shell was going to knock the old house in which I was sleeping. We arrived in gay Paris in the early evening. It was beautiful to get into a bed with clean sheets and no shelling.

The next day we took a trip to Versailles, the Palace of the King (Louis XIV). The place is beyond description and I leave the postcards sent to give you an idea of the architecture and beautiful gardens and surroundings of the place. In Paris they have two meatless days a week and subsist on eggs, etc. France is a funny place. Tipping is a curse, in many places the employe pays the employer for the privilege of working for him. Waiters must be tipped 10 per cent of the value purchased. They are not at all backward either, and even ask for it, letting one know when the tip is insufficient.

Paris is on war bread made in loaves about 2ft. long and six inches round. They buy their bread by the yard, so to speak. The trams are electric and resemble young trains.

We met two Australian girls. One is on hospital war work, and she made herself known and took dinner with us, afterwards we went to a "magasin" *[shop]* and bought blouses etc, distinctly Parisian, for some girl friends in Australia. Inside the place is like a big theatre with beautiful decorations, paintings and paperings most gorgeous. The departments are on floors (six or seven around the sides like galleries with a most magnificent dome in the centre.) French girls do know how to dress and they look most charming and becoming. They are very lively and impress a foreigner very much indeed. They will make a dress from practically nothing, but pay great attention to head dress or feet.

The other Australian girl is an artist, and we took tea at her studio and had quite a good time. Here we met a Russian girl, a nice little French madame, a Canadian lady, and two Canadian soldiers.

The theatres are of the music hall variety, and there is a promenade at the back where people can walk round while the show is in progress. We "fell' in the first day by taking a guide. Afterwards we met an Englishman who knows Paris very well and he took us about.

In France if a man pays by cheque and he has NSF *[not sufficient funds]* he is fined. I have also been told that if a person gets run over by a taxi he, and not the taxi driver, is fined for being too slow. I do not vouch for the truth of it. The taxis go along at some rate and twist about and pull up dead sudden, avoiding collisions by a fraction every minute of the day. I am now prepared to go back to the trenches for a rest. These days have been so busy and full that there has been little time for sleep. It has been worth while. I have not heard anything from Roy *[brother]* since I returned to France. He is still in England and quite well, and enjoying life immensely."

October 18 1917
(Letter received November 15, 1917)
Letter received last mail by his parents from Lt Ernest Jesse Joseph Hooper mentions having met Roy Gollan from the 'Advertiser' in London. When they were walking along Queen's Road, they met Ernie Sabeston from the *[Geelong]* Savings Bank.

Lt Hooper has just completed a 2-month course for officers chosen to command a company in battle. He has since proceeded to France.* Captain Gollan has also completed a staff course at Cambridge.

* Not long after Hooper's letter was received, he was killed in action at Bourlon Wood, France.

Mr Gollan received a cable message from his son Lt Robert Gollan, stating he has been wounded by a bullet in the back — "Slight. Doing well. Blighty."

This is the second occasion on which he has been injured. His brother, Roy, has received appointment as Captain and is attached to General Elliott's Headquarters staff, 15th Infantry Brigade. He was well at time of writing (18th October 1917).

Tally: published in 'News of the Week' December 16, 1917

Geelong and Western District Soldiers
Casualty List No 359 contained 1166 names, comprised of —
Killed in action 59, died of wounds 24, died other causes 1, wounded 998, missing 36, sick 43, injured 5, prisoners of war 3. (Robert Gollan was included in this list.)

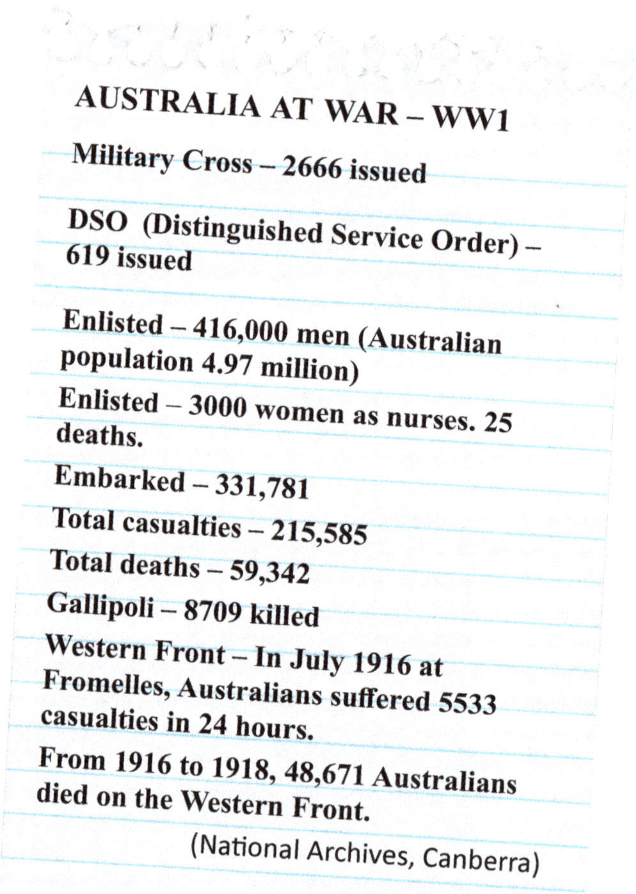

AUSTRALIA AT WAR – WW1

Military Cross – 2666 issued

DSO (Distinguished Service Order) – 619 issued

Enlisted – 416,000 men (Australian population 4.97 million)

Enlisted – 3000 women as nurses. 25 deaths.

Embarked – 331,781

Total casualties – 215,585

Total deaths – 59,342

Gallipoli – 8709 killed

Western Front – In July 1916 at Fromelles, Australians suffered 5533 casualties in 24 hours.

From 1916 to 1918, 48,671 Australians died on the Western Front.

(National Archives, Canberra)

'Cobbers' was installed in the Australian Memorial Park at Fromelles in 1998.

Roy Gollan's service medals, from left: Distinguished Service Order, Military Cross, 1914-15 Star, British War Medal and Victory Medal.

HERBERT ROY GOLLAN ~ BRIGADE MAJOR WAR RECORD

War Service Medals

- Companion of the Distinguished Service Order (DSO)
- Military Cross – June 13, 1918 (Front line)
- Mentioned in Despatches (twice)
- British War Medal
- Victory Medal and Oak Leaf Cluster
- Anzac Commemorative Medallion – Gallipoli Service (issued 1967)
- 1914 -15 Star – Overseas Service

Brief History of Roy's War Service

- 19-10-1914 Signed Loyal Oath in Melbourne and subsequently joined up. 3rd Light Horse Brigade. Corporal. Aged 22 years. Occupation: Journalist
- 16-5-1915   Embarked from Alexandria for Gallipoli on ship 'Menominee'
- 21-9-1915   Typhoid. Hospital Gallipoli Peninsula. Then hospital Malta with enteric fever (typhoid).

- 25-10-1915 Embarked for England on Hospital Ship 'Oxfordshire'
- 22-2-1916 Returned to duty, Egypt. 54th Battalion
- 44-10-1916 Proceeded to France as Lieutenant
- 24-1-1917 Gunshot wound right pectoral. Admitted 8-2-1917 London General Hospital
- 24-3-1917 Rejoined Unit in France
- 14-7-1917 Staff Course at Clare College, Cambridge. Seconded to 5th Aust. Div. HQ as Staff Captain
- 22-4-1918 Seconded as Brigade Major in France. Rejoined Unit, 15th Infantry Brigade
- 4-6-1918 Awarded Military Cross. London Gazette, 3-6-1918
- Course at Grantham, England
- 31-12-1918 Mentioned in despatches. AIF Decoration
- 3-6-1919 Awarded the DSO
- 4-6-1919 Granted leave — reason: Journalist for 'Argus' and 'Australasian', Fleet Street, London.
- 19-6-1919 Return to Australia. Awarded MSO, Mentioned in Sir Douglas Haig's despatch 16-3-1919

Later service
- 1-10-1920 Captain
- 21-8-1928 Major

Reasons for Awards

From CEW Bean's 'Official History of Australia in the War of 1914–1918':
"8-9 August, 1915, France.
Canadian Brigade Major asked if Australian division could help to attack an open flank.... Captain Gollan rushed to the two support battalions ... then [proceeded] with an order to leapfrog the two front battalions and attack... Tanks expected but didn't come to support."

From diary of 6th Canadian Infantry Brigadier: "Their prompt and generous action enabled our assault to proceed in this initial stage and saved us numerous casualties."

Roy's records say he showed gallantry and exceptional service. Elsewhere it is noted that he showed exceptional organisational abilities and the ability to get a good response from men. He certainly did achieve rapid promotion.

> George the Fifth, by the Grace of God of the United Kingdom of Great Britain and Ireland and of the British Dominions beyond the Seas, King, Defender of the Faith, Emperor of India, Sovereign of the Distinguished Service Order, to our Trusty and Well beloved Herbert Roy Gollan Esquire M.C., Captain in the Forces of Our Commonwealth of Australia Greeting
>
> Whereas We have thought fit to Nominate and Appoint you to be a Member of our Distinguished Service Order We do by these Presents Grant unto you the Dignity of a Companion of Our said Order And we do hereby authorize you to Have, Hold and Enjoy the said Dignity as a Member of Our said Order, together with all and singular the Privileges thereunto belonging or appertaining.
>
> Given at Our Court at St James's under Our Sign Manual this Third day of June 1919 in the Ninth Year of our Reign.
>
> By The Sovereign's Command
>
> Captain H. R. Gollan
> 56th Battalion
> Australian Infantry
>
> The Principal Secretary of State having the Department of War for the time being

Copy of DSO award dated June 3, 1919

The following has no connection with the Gollan brothers; however, the author appeared often in the 'Geelong Advertiser' writing on spiritual matters, and it is an interesting reflection on love, religion and brotherhood in wartime. It was published in the 'Advertiser' on March 9, 1918.

IN A HOSPITAL WARD
By William McIntosh

Allan McDonald had felt the call of war. He looked upon it as unreasonable, he who had known nothing worse in Nature than the fight of the bullocks, but the idea so obsessed him that he could think of nothing else.

Finally, he told his old mother that he had made up his mind to enlist. Instead of breaking down and expostulating, all she said was, "God bless you Allan, I've expected this."

Three weeks later he had fixed up things at their little selection in the wilds of Gippsland and donned the khaki. Hadn't his own forefathers gathered to their chief's call centuries before as his Grannie had told him in his early days? Then why should he refuse now that the spirit of the warrior haunted him, and his country needed his services? The breadwinner dying early, the widow had struggled on with the boys' and a neighbour's help now and then, to keep the place going, and finally succeeded till it paid itself fairly well. His scanty education, given by his parents, had been enriched by a deep study of the Book of Nature, and his religious training might have been summed up in his mother's favourite maxim: "Trust in God and do the right," for in their forest isolation he had learned nothing of catechism, or creed, or prayer book.

Plunged suddenly into the maelstrom of camp life, the revelation it gave him came as a shock to his simple and open mind, and the cunning depths of many of these city chaps around him were a sore puzzle to him.

Six months later he was through a severe action in France and got wounded, but he managed to reach the nearest dressing station, bringing in a badly wounded German on his back, while he had crawled on his stomach all the way with the load. When bantered about fetching an enemy, he replied that he died not know one skin from another; all he knew was that a fellow creature was in trouble and needed help.

Fate laid him in a hospital bed in St Thomas's, overlooking the Thames and the Houses of Parliament, and next to a youth of 25 from the backblocks of North Queensland….they soon chummed up. The latter, like McDonald, was a child of the bush, lean and tall, and wiry as rubber. He was full of life and playful as a kitten. Reared on a station far in the interior, he had known nothing but cattle and horses, with a weekly or fortnightly visit to the homestead, where a brief intercourse with the other station hands awakened his soul from its torpor.

The two bedmates, thrown thus strangely together, opened their souls to each other, finding delight in their mutual interchanges. He had seen but two weeks of trench life when he got hit in the foot so badly that the surgeon said it might have to come off, but the patient didn't mind; in fact, nothing seemed to matter to him if he could be of any service to others.

Because of his height and wiriness they had dubbed him Long Gum, but as he pleasantly rejoined, if it pleased them better than his own name, Gilfellan, then it pleased him. It was the simplicity and manly outspokenness that warmed him to his campmates, while his ignorance of the world and its devious ways amused them greatly. He was a genuine child of the bush, every horse nearby was his favourite, and if a stray dog or goat got into camp it and Long Gum drew to each other as naturally as needles to magnet, and stuck as close.

The first week he was in hospital one of the doctors, noticing his healthy constitution and great vitality, asked him, more in jest than earnest, if he had any blood he could spare. Long Gum told him he could have a pint or two of his any time if it would save a patient's life, and the doctor got no peace until he had effected the transfusion to a sinking patient, thus setting him on the mend. When the medical man ventured the remark to the nurse that "if our hero had known his foot would have to be amputated he would probably not have parted so readily with his blood," her reply surprised him. "Make no mistake, doctor, it would not have made the slightest difference. He is one of the 'Gritty Australians'."

The Parson who visited them was sorely puzzled. What could he do with a couple of barbarians who had not been baptised, knew nothing of the creeds or sacraments, and had only heard the name of Jesus Christ when associated with profanity. The quizzical feeling was as strong in the bushman as it was on the cleric's part, for after *[the parson left]* one day, McDonald beckoned his companion to draw his wheelchair closer and remarked, "What is this 'ere salvation he is always yabbing about?"

"Wants us to get saved badly, and get a clear passport to Heaven." I sez to him, 'Look 'ere Guv'nor, if you can show me a better passport to the heavenly mansions than a clean life, with sacrifice for its keynote, I'd like to see it.' He hummed and muttered something about the necessity of believing on the Lord and being baptised, and that even sacrificing one's life on the battlefield wouldn't save a fellow from eternal punishment.

"I jerked in 'Will you explain this eternal punishment to us?' And would you believe it mate, when he had done I was as red in the face as a turkey cock at the horror of it, and all I could say was 'Mister Parson, if that's your religion, give me my dog's, for his is a bit more human and genuine. There's deep gratitude in my faithful collie, and there was the same in my heart to him. When we served each other in the wilds it was out of love to each other, and if love is not the basis of sacrifice, I dunno what is. I guess it's love of dear old England that brought us twelve thousand miles to fight on her behalf, for downtrodden Belgium and France." "Ay, an' for dear old Australia too, matey," chimed in McDonald, "for heaven help us if Britain fails. Ours is the richest prize in the market."

McDonald, though he well knew his days were numbered, spoke with great earnestness, and sank back apparently exhausted.

Said Long Gum, resuming, "I've carried a blackfellow five miles to our shanty after they had attacked us, and he had broke his leg; but it was nothing more than one man would do for another. We tended him till he got right and could walk away, but he'd hardly leave us. We were never troubled by blacks again, and he cried like a child when he had to go."

"Children of Nature, they are just like our faithful dogs," added McDonald.

"This fellow," resumed Long Gum, "told us all about their ways of living and their religion, for they had plenty of it. Their morality, too, was cleaner than most of the whites'. I've heard father say, and as they had no contact with white races till we came on the scene, it follows they had their own natural religion. They worshipped the Great Spirit in their own way, but the revelation of the future life came direct from those of their tribes who had crossed the river of death. Each tribe had its own spokesman, or medicine man; but they had no sacred books to hand down for centuries. The Great Spirit was their Father and their All."

"Well, Allan, they say you've not long to live, and maybe you can't swallow this stuff the parson gives us, but I think we are agreed that the blackfellow's religion is more suited to our souls than this British-grown article we can't understand, and it won't bear grafting either.

"I know a truer-hearted woman the Creator never made than my mother, and her religion was summed up in one sentence: 'Trust in God and do the right.' It did for me during the worst six months I've seen — soldiering; but for it I'd have been lower than the beasts, and I've seen some men lower when we picked them up.

"When I asked the Padre what became of the millions of blacks that had peopled the big island continent of ours for hundreds, maybe thousands, of years, unmolested, he admitted with a sigh they would be lost, according to the teaching of the Church."

"Well, friend," interjected McDonald solemnly, "if that's the Church's teaching, I wouldn't give much for its chance of being saved, as he calls it."

"I told him," said Long Gum, "about that handsome lady, dressed all in black, who visited us last week and hearing that we were Australians, she stayed an hour reading to us choice extracts from 'great authors', she called them, and they were good. One she repeated several times. I remember she said it was the Nazarene's, but I never asked who he was. It ran 'He that doeth the will of My Father in Heaven, the same is My brother, My sister and mother.' I had heard Mother say that years agone, so it came back fresh and familiar."

"I'm quite agreed with you, mate, an' if I never get up, as there seems small chance of doing, I'll pass out in peace and trust, knowing He doeth all things well."

A week later a small procession left St Thomas's and wended its way past the old Lambeth Palace of the Archbishops, up by the Thames towards Twickenham. The chief mourner was was a one-legged soldier, Gilfillan, alias Long Gum. Of his late chum, Allan McDonald, he could say that he was truly faithful in all his dealings, and if he saw not that dear mother's face he had left afar, he knew, aye, he knew from his inmost soul, he would not have long to wait to welcome her in the great home beyond. By his light he had done his best, and had no fear of the future.

"Lay me," he said, "where I can still see the flowers blooming in the meadows and the lambs gambol in the springrime, and I'll be content to try and help some of those I've knocked against from falling into the pit of shame — content to serve in this way — till she come."

* * *

Lone Pine before the charge at Gallipoli

Roy Gollan, Light Horse Brigade.

AUSTRALIAN WAR MEMORIAL

Roy Gollan (far left) with Brigadier-General H.E. Elliot (pointing) and Major-General J.J. Talbot Hobbs during a Light Horse review at the village of Huppy on the Somme in France, October 29, 1918.

Roy and Muriel on their wedding day, 1920. Before her marriage Muriel Hyatt was a music teacher in Bendigo.

Housebreaker Surprised.

WOMAN'S STARTLING EXPERIENCE.

INTRUDER THREATENS HER WITH A REVOLVER.

The police authorities have not yet succeeded in locating the daring housebreaker who was surprised by Mrs. H. R. Gollan in the grounds of her home in Howitt-road, East St. Kilda, late on Tuesday afternoon.

Returning to her house at about 4 p.m., Mrs. Gollan was surprised to find the side gate and the back door open. On entering the dwelling she found the rooms in a state of disorder. They had evidently been ransacked, as clothing and jewellery to the value of £40 were missing. After finding that the house had been robbed Mrs. Gollan walked into the back yard, with the intention of reporting the matter to the police, when she was confronted by a man hiding in the fernery. She asked "What are you doing here?" Without replying the man backed away, and Mrs. Gollan proceeded to follow him. Thereupon he produced a revolver, and levelling it at her exclaimed, "Don't move, or I'll shoot." Then he scaled a broken fence and escaped. The man gained entrance to the house by forcing a side window with a chisel.

Drama for Muriel when a burglar pointed a gun at her at their Melbourne home in 1924.

The Age, 4 December 1924

A LIFE IN INDIA: ROY GOLLAN

Muriel and Roy Gollan

High Indian Office Filled

CANBERRA, Tuesday.—Mr H. R. Gollan has been appointed Australian High Commissioner in India.

He succeeds Sir Iven MacKay, who returned to Australia in June after completion of his term of office.

Mr. Gollan has been senior Australian Government Trade Commissioner in Bombay since 1939.

October 6 1948

1949: H R Gollan, as High Commissioner, reads a message from the Australian Prime Minister (Robert Menzies) to the Maharajah of Nepal.

Official photo with the Maharajah on visit to Nepal to present his credentials, 1949

Acknowledging the salute, Nepal 1949

Attending the swearing in of the Indian President, Rajendra Prasad, in 1950.

At home in New Delhi

Above: Muriel Gollan poses with the staff member known as the 'head boy', and his wife, and at right, the couple with all the household staff.

Former Journalist Becomes India High Commissioner

CANBERRA, Tuesday. — Appointment of Mr. Herbert Roy Gollan as Australian High Commissioner in India was announced today by the Prime Minister (Mr. Chifley).

He succeeds Sir Iven Mackay, who returned to Australia in June, after completing his term of office.

Mr. Gollan has been senior Australian Government Trade Commissioner in Bombay since 1938 and has also acted as commercial counsellor to the Australian High Commissioner.

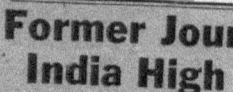
Mr. H. R. Gollan

Mr. Gollan was a journalist and, after serving in the 1914-18 War became manager of the Victorian Government Tourist Bureau.

He was Indian representative of the Australian National Travel Association before his appointment as Trade Commissioner.

Former Jour[nalist Becomes] India High [Commissioner]

CANBERRA, Tuesday. — Roy Gollan as Aust[ralian High Commissioner in] India was announced t[oday by the Prime Minister] (Mr. Chifley).

He succeeds Sir Iven Mackay, who returned to Australia in June, after completing his term of office.

Mr. Gollan has been senior Australian Government Trade Commissioner in Bombay since 1938 and has also acted as commercial counsellor to the Australian High Commissioner.

Mr. H. R. Gollan

Mr. Gollan was a journalist and, after serving in the 1914-18 War became manager of the Victorian Government Tourist Bureau.

He was Indian representative of the Australian National Travel Association before his appointment as Trade Commissioner.

Newsman and Diplomat: Mr. Roy Gollan Dies at 75

A famous Bendigonian, Mr. Herbert Roy Gollan, D.S.O., M.C., has died in Melbourne in his 76th year. Educated at Bendigo Central School, Mr. Gollan had a distinguished career in newspaper and diplomatic circles.

Mr. Gollan was a First World War veteran, serving in Gallipoli, Sinai, France and Belgium. He was originally with the Eighth Light Horse and transferred in 1915 to the 58th Battalion as captain and finally became adjutant of the 54th Battalion.

He joined a staff course at Clare College, Cambridge, and became staff captain and brigade major of the 15th Infantry Brigade.

He was decorated with the Military Cross in 1918 and the D.S.O. in 1919. He was also mentioned three times in dispatches.

Mr. Gollan became manager of the Victorian Government Tourist Bureau in 1926, and went to the Melbourne Argus as assistant manager in 1928. He was managing editor of the Melbourne Star from 1933-36, and manager of the Argus from 1936-37.

He became Australian Government Trade Commissioner in India from 1939 to 1948 and then spent another four years as Australian High Commissioner in India.

While in India he was representative of the Australian National Publicity Association and for a period was the Australian member of the Eastern Group Supply Council.

In 1920 he married Miss Murial Hyett, of Bendigo. She survives her husband.

Mr. Gollan had recently resided at Kings Road, Emerald. His funeral to Springvale took place yesterday.

AUSTRALIA'S fir[st Com]missioner in In[dia, Mr.] Gollan, has now est[ablished] quarters in Calcutta. [The post was] created by the Federal Government because of the increasing importance of Australia's trade with India.

Mr. Gollan. knows India well, was formerly manager there for Australian National Travel Association, and is keen to develop this new contact.

MR. H. ROY GOLLAN represents the Australian National Travel Association in India. The Association is out to develop Australia's tourist traffic.

July 1937

GOLLAN, Herbert Roy, D.S.O. 1919; M.C. 1918; b. 29 Aug. 1892; s. of Robert Harper Gollan and Harriet Wilson; m. 1920; no c. Educ.: Central School, Bendigo. Served with Hamilton Spectator and Geelong Advertiser; enlisted with Australian Imperial Force, Oct. 1914; served till Nov. 1919; Adjutant 54th Infantry Batt., Staff Captain 15th Infantry Brigade, and later Brigade Major (D.S.O., M.C., wounded, despatches thrice); Manager Victorian Government Tourist Bureau, 1923-28; Manager, The Argus and The Australasian, 1928-1937; Australian Government Trade Commissioner in India, 1939. Delegate to Eastern Group Supply Conference, 1941;

Early 'Geelong Avertiser' office

The *Geelong Advertiser* was first published on
21 November 1840.
It is the oldest continuing newspaper title in
Victoria and the second-oldest in Australia. The
Advertiser regularly dedicated full pages to
soldiers' letters home.

www.ingramcontent.com/pod-product-compliance
Lightning Source LLC
Chambersburg PA
CBHW061154010526
44118CB00027B/2972